Property of the King

From Possession to Divine Redemption

Deborah Mckinzie

Copyright © 2023 Deborah Mckinzie, All rights reserved.

Property of the King, or any portion thereof may not be reproduced or used in any manner whatsoever without the express written permission of the publisher except for the use of brief quotations in a book review.

Printed in the United States of America

Cover Illustration and Design By: Stacy Hooker
Edited By: Dawn Carter

First Printing, United States of America, October 2023

ISBN: 979-8-9890655-0-9 (Paperback)

ISBN 979-8-9890655-1-6 (eBook)

Property of the King

1 3 5 7 9 10 8 6 4 2

This book is dedicated to my husband Johnny. My ride or die. I love you more!

Contents

1. Boundless Spirits: Adventurous Hearts. — 1
2. Riding the Winds of Change — 9
3. Climbing the Ladder — 18
4. Stepping Up — 27
5. Welcome to a New World — 32
6. Seen Not Heard — 38
7. Accelerating Bonds — 46
8. Unexpected Conversations — 55
9. Momma of the House — 75
10. God's Unrelenting Pursuit — 83
11. Embracing the Light in the Darkness — 94
12. Deception — 98
13. God's Saving Grace — 114
14. Forgiveness Is a Beautiful Thing — 126
15. Never Going Back — 138
16. Living in the Light — 149

Photo Gallery	160
From the Author	168
About the Author	170
Acknowledgments	172

Chapter One

Boundless Spirits: Adventurous Hearts.

"Trust in the Lord with all your heart and lean not on your own understanding; in all your ways submit to Him, and He will make your paths straight." ~Proverbs 3.5-6 (NIV)

WITH MY HANDS ON my hips, my eight-year-old self asked my auntie, "What are we going to do now? I'm bored." The day started with my uncle loading a rented van with seven of my cousins, my brother, and myself, heading to Six Flags Great America, an amusement park in Gurnee, Illinois. It was a bold move for my uncle, considering he didn't have any children of his own. Despite the stress of temporarily losing my brother for a bit, the excitement that day remains etched in my memory as a truly remarkable one. Water rides, roller coasters, and an unlimited supply of candy made it an unforgettable adventure.

There's one thing about me that hasn't changed much over the years—I've always seemed to have an excess of energy. Even as an eight-year-old, I couldn't sit still for more than a few minutes without dozing off. To this day, at the age of 52, the same tendency persists. It's like a switch flips, and I'm instantly asleep if I'm not in motion. But the moment I wake up, I'm charged and ready to go. Unfortunately, the rest of my family didn't share the same instantaneous recharge ability.

My cousins and my brother, worn out from the day's adventures, were completely drained of energy.

Once again, I repeated my question, "What are we going to do now?" My auntie shook her head in amazement, clearly astonished by my endless well of energy, and inquired about when my parents would be picking me up. She was exhausted.

Little did I know that my life would continue to unfold in a similar manner even as I grew older. People have always said that I have too much energy for one person. I can't tell you how many times I heard my mother say, "Thank God she's not a twin." I've never thought my energy was a problem. In fact, I've always found it exhilarating. Energy is the fuel that propels me forward, enabling me to pursue all the things I want to do. For example, it has driven me across the finish line of grueling hundred-mile trail races I've competed in. It has opened a clothing boutique. It created a photography business. This kind of energy even helped when I started a 501c3 charity that provided shoes and socks for children in need.

While some have labeled it as attention deficit disorder (ADD), I prefer to think of it as an abundance of energy waiting to be unleashed.

Over time, I've learned to harness and channel my energy, making it work for me rather than letting it overwhelm me as it's done in the past. Age has brought me wisdom and understanding, teaching me how to control and direct this inherent power I have. I've discovered ways to navigate this boundless power within me, using it to my advantage in all aspects of life.

My parents often struggled with my boundless bursts of energy and adventurous spirit. Despite the challenges, they remained dedicated to supporting me throughout my high school years. Tutors, extra-credit assignments, and detentions became a regular part of my academic journey. When the time came for me to graduate, I eagerly dashed across the stage, seizing my diploma from the principal's hand. Amidst the cheers of my classmates, I could hear their playful remark, "Better check to see if it's signed, Deb."

My high school counselor, with a condescending tone, stated that my grades were inadequate for admission to a university and proposed that I attend cosmetology school instead. He made it clear that he believed it was the best option available to me. Furthermore, he cautioned me that I might need to take on a second job to support myself. According to him, hairdressers were not renowned for earning substantial incomes. He even insinuated that my best chance for financial security might be to marry someone who could provide for me.

Working in my aunt's salon during my formative years had a profound impact on me. I always had a great time there, and witnessing the success my aunt achieved inspired me. She became a remarkable mentor for me, showcasing the possibilities within the beauty industry. Despite the counselor's lack of encouragement, I decided to take his advice.

Looking back, I can proudly say that I defied the odds. I exceeded my own expectations and flourished in the realm of hairstyling. It wasn't just about proving the counselor wrong; it was about embracing an opportunity, following my passion, and carving a fulfilling path for myself. Cosmetology school was just the beginning of a remarkable journey that allowed me to create my own success and shape a life that resembled the achievements of my inspirational auntie.

After receiving my hairdressing license from the state of Michigan and pursuing my big dreams in the beauty industry, finding myself pregnant was definitely not part of the plan. It was a bewildering situation because, given my severe endometriosis, my doctor informed me that the chances of conceiving were extremely slim. Yet, there I stood, holding the home pregnancy test that boldly displayed two bright red lines.

My cousin Terra, by my side in my parent's kitchen, asked me the question I was already grappling with, "What are you going to do?" It was as if she needed confirmation of what seemed undeniable. "You're pregnant."

The immediate thought that crossed my mind was the fear of my parents' reaction. "My parents are going to kill me!" I exclaimed. The lofty dreams I had envisioned for myself would have to be put on hold. I now had a new and unexpected adventure awaiting me. Despite the circumstances, I felt an overwhelming excitement for the little bundle of joy who would soon join me in this world. I couldn't wait.

As my pregnancy progressed, my boyfriend transformed into my husband. Though initially reluctant to marry, he likely felt compelled to do the right thing as we faced the impending arrival of our child. I, too, felt the pressure to make amends for getting pregnant before marriage. Perhaps, in some way, I thought that by marrying the father of our child before his birth, I could rectify the perceived sin of premarital sex. It was my attempt to fulfill the expectations of being the good Roman Catholic girl my mom had hoped for. We were married a few months after, as if it would somehow set things right in the eyes of the Lord.

PROPERTY OF THE KING

You might expect that being pregnant would naturally slow me down and drain my energy, but surprisingly, that wasn't the case for me. Even two weeks past my due date, with a large belly, I went about my usual tasks with determination. And so it happened that while cutting the grass on a late July day, I suddenly went into labor.

Twenty-five grueling hours of intense labor followed. Through every contraction and moment of exhaustion, I pushed forward, eagerly awaiting the arrival of our precious son. And finally, after all the pain and effort, he was placed into my loving arms.

At 21, I found myself married with a precious baby and working at my aunt's salon, conveniently living just a block away from my parents' house. While my physical distance hadn't taken me far, my dreams and aspirations for the future knew no bounds. However, the responsibilities and pressures of adult life began to weigh heavily on me. As I tried to keep up with societal expectations, the bills started piling up, and cracks appeared in my marriage. Beyond the joy of motherhood, something felt wrong. This wasn't the picture-perfect dream I had envisioned for my life.

I yearned for adventure and romance, craving a life that was vibrant and filled with possibilities. Meanwhile, my husband seemed content with a more sedate existence, finding joy in napping while I yearned to explore the world around me. In pursuit of my passion, I started attending hair shows with my friends from the salon, captivated by the industry's professionals showcasing their skills on stage. I looked forward to the time that I could become an educator for product companies, sharing my knowledge and creativity with others.

Eventually, the disconnection in our paths became evident, and my husband and I made the difficult decision to end our marriage after a few short years. While it was a challenging period, I knew deep down that I had to follow my own desires and aspirations, even if meant starting over.

A NEW LOVE BECKONS: EMBRACING LIFE'S UNEXPECTED ADVENTURES

I didn't remain single for long. I first encountered John at a hair show in Stevens Point, Wisconsin, and our love story commenced like a fairy tale. It was a collision of worlds, with a rebellious spirit from Los Angeles crossing paths with an innocent girl from a small town. Although our relationship was initially long-distance, we despised being apart. Following my separation, I moved into a modest apartment above my grandfather's house with my son. There were concerns that I might relocate to Los Angeles to be with John, but I realized the significance of keeping our son in the same town as his father and our extended families. This left John with a decision to abandon his established success in LA and embrace a life with me in the Yoop (Upper Peninsula of Michigan, as it is fondly known). He packed his belongings into a compact U-Haul and embarked on a cross-country journey to be by my side. Prior to cohabitating, I wanted to ensure we did things right this time. John explored numerous housing options before selecting a renovated school building. His apartment just so happened to be my fourth-grade classroom.

PROPERTY OF THE KING

The first item to roll off the U-Haul upon John's arrival was his most prized possession—a FLH Shovelhead Harley Davidson. After all, the bad boy in our fairy tale needed a bike. Little did I know at that moment how significantly this motorcycle would shape our future.

A few months after John settled in, I went to court to finalize my first marriage. Later that evening, John and I planned to dine at one of our favorite restaurants, intending to commemorate the end of that chapter in my life. Little did I realize; our celebration would also mark our engagement—an unexpected twist of fate.

We exchanged vows a few months later in a courthouse wedding, with two small receptions to follow.

John's family thought he was out of his mind for leaving his lucrative career in Hollywood to start anew in a small town with me. But they recognized that this was precisely what he needed to maintain the sobriety he had achieved two years prior to meeting me.

John and I engaged in numerous conversations about his past addiction, delving into the depths of what it was like and how he was navigating his recovery. We both agreed that substance abuse had no place in our lives together. I made it abundantly clear that I would not tolerate it, emphasizing that it would be a surefire way to jeopardize and ultimately destroy our marriage. In the early stages of our relationship, I felt anxious about the possibility of a relapse, but as timed passed, those worries gradually faded away. Perhaps I became complacent and somewhat forgetful of the life he had led before me. While I experimented with prescription pills and alcohol during my college years, I convinced myself that they were sanctioned by medical doctors and legally available, making them distinct from the illicit nature of street drugs. The foundation of our understanding was simple yet firm—John achieved sobriety, and he comprehended the dire consequences he would face if he ever chose to return to substance use. He knew exactly what was at stake: the life and family we were building together. I made it explicitly clear from the beginning how I would react if he strayed from the path of sobriety.

After settling into our new location, we wasted no time in diving headfirst into our endeavors. With perseverance, we purchased a home and embarked on establishing the area's very first full-day spa and salon. Simultaneously, we were fully engaged in the exhilarating journey of parenthood, which proved to be an adventure in and of itself.

In our own unique way, we defined our success and achieved it. We shared the same adventurous spirit and boundless energy, finally finding someone who could keep up with each other's pace. Our creative minds and spontaneity always drove us to seek the next big thing, constantly craving novelty and excitement. Professionally, we were on the right track, while our social lives were filled with excitement. We navigated life together, learning and growing with each passing day.

Chapter Two

Riding the Winds of Change

"But those who hope in the Lord will renew their strength. They will soar on wings like eagles; they will run and not grow weary, they will walk and not be faint." ~ Isaiah 40:31 (NIV)

After John and I tied the knot, he quickly embraced the Yooper lifestyle, or at least as much as an outsider could. The locals have their own criteria for who can truly be called a Yooper, with some insisting that you have to be born here while others believe that enduring seven consecutive winters earns you the title. Having survived his first winter in our little corner of the world, John was eager to dust off his Harley and hit the road.

Enter my cousin, Wahoo, the President of a local motorcycle club. Wahoo and I have always shared a close bond, so it was no surprise when he extended an invitation for John to join the club on their next ride. John returned home buzzing with excitement, eager to meet these guys and explore the scenic wonders of his new home. The ride proved to be an exhilarating experience for John, fueling his enthusiasm to attend his first club meeting.

At the time, the club was a riding club, a group of longtime riders who relished the freedom of the open road. They reveled in the joy of the wind caressing their faces and the sun warming their backs. Beyond their love for riding, this club had also established a commendable reputation for their charitable endeavors in our community. Their commitment to giving back garnered respect and admiration from locals.

My cousin had given me a ride on his bike a couple times in the past, but his daredevil nature always made me a bit nervous as a passenger. He was the kind of rider who fearlessly popped wheelies on his fully dressed bagger motorcycle, effortlessly cruising for a block on one wheel. I always knew he was involved with a club of some sort, but it didn't hold much significance for me until John started riding alongside him.

This particular club had a relaxed and flexible structure, with my cousin not exactly running a tight ship. He aimed to have a good time and bring in new friends and members to expand the club's camaraderie and shared adventures. Their motto was simple: more riders, more fun.

After a few exhilarating rides with the club, John decided to become an official member. I was thrilled for him and looked forward to joining him on the back of his bike. It was a fantastic opportunity for him to connect with new friends. With our days already consumed by working together at the salon, I understood the need for him to have an outlet of his own. As a busy mom and salon owner, my time was limited, and that was perfectly fine.

Soon after joining the club, John brought his experience and knowledge from a more structured motorcycle club in Los Angeles to this small-town group of riders. He proposed some changes, aiming for a more serious and organized approach. This led my cousin, Wahoo, to step down from his role as president, as he simply didn't have the time required to fulfill the position under the new vision. The club held a vote, and a new president, someone we both respected and admired, was elected.

With the decision to transition from a riding club to an organized motorcycle club, significant changes were in store. Not everyone in the club embraced these changes wholeheartedly. Some preferred to maintain the old ways, while others were excited about the potential for growth and development. I witnessed newfound confidence in some of the members, a transformation I hadn't seen before. If they thought they were tough guys before, they certainly lived up to that image now, especially my husband.

The introduction of new by-laws brought about a more structured approach, ensuring that members adhered to the rules and regulations. It wasn't as simple as it once was, merely contributing a hundred bucks and riding an American-built bike. These changes demanded a greater commitment, and John embraced them wholeheartedly. The evolution of the club became his passion, and he thrived in the midst of the transformation.

It was a tight-knit family, bound by a shared love for the open road and the thrill of riding. Our fellow brothers and sisters in the club were more than just riding companions; they were cherished friends who embraced the same sense of adventure. We relished the uncertainty of our journeys, often setting off without a predetermined destination. That sense of spontaneity brought us immense joy.

John was a part of this club for years, and through our involvement, we had the pleasure of meeting countless incredible individuals. I forged strong friendships with the wives and girlfriends of the bikers, often referred to as old ladies. We spent a great deal of time together, forming a supportive community within the motorcycle club.

Although women were allowed to ride their own bikes on group rides, we were not considered official members of this club. It was a men's club. That didn't deter us from looking out for one another. When someone was going through a difficult time, we rallied together to offer support and find solutions. If an old lady was facing challenges, the other women in the club would stand by her side.

I vividly recall a heartbreaking situation involving a close friend who discovered her husband's infidelity. I became her confidante, lending a listening ear as she poured out her pain and tears. While I wished she would leave him, she made the decision to remain in the marriage under the condition that he could continue seeing other women. It wasn't a choice I agreed with, but it wasn't my place to make that decision for her. Throughout the years of her suffering, I stood by her side, providing love and support.

Within the motorcycle club, there was an unspoken club among the women. We even had our own unique lady patches symbolizing our connection and unity. Such a distinction was not seen in the higher-ranking clubs of the motorcycle world, and some members within our club even questioned its validity. However, our men knew where their loyalties lay, and our families always came first. Family life took precedence, followed by work, and then the club.

In this special corner of the motorcycle community, we found strength, friendship, and unwavering support. We were united by a bond that extended beyond the thrill of riding, forming a sisterhood that weathered the challenges of life together.

As a strong and confident woman, I never found myself to feel belittled or inferior in the motorcycle club by men. Fortunately, most men within this club held a deep respect for women.

We were asked to contribute by cooking and cleaning at parties. It never felt demeaning or disrespectful. In fact, I felt appreciated by the men for my efforts. It was a way for me to contribute and be part of the camaraderie.

I couldn't ignore the dynamics among some of the old ladies within the sisterhood. There was an unwritten expectation for us to participate in preparations and cleanup. Failure to do so often resulted in harsh judgment and gossip from other old ladies, not so much the men. Some women could be particularly cruel and mean-spirited towards one another. It seemed that a few old ladies were shouldering the majority of the work most of the time, and this caused problems among us.

It became clear to me that there were certain expectations and roles within this predominantly male club. If you happened to be enjoying yourself at the bar while other old ladies were working, it was frowned upon. This was a subtle reminder of where women were positioned within this male-dominated space. Those who didn't conform to these expectations were swiftly reminded of their place.

While it was disheartening to witness this dynamic, it was also an awakening for me, a realization of the gender dynamics at play in a club primarily composed of men. It highlighted the importance of asserting oneself and finding a balance between participating and challenging the status quo. I refused to be confined to predefined roles and expectations, striving to carve out my own place within the club while standing up for equal respect and recognition from both men and women.

RANKS: THE HIERARCHY OF PATCH-WEARING CLUBS

In the hierarchy of the motorcycle club, John held the esteemed position of sergeant at arms. With unwavering dedication, he assumed the role of maintaining order, enforcing club protocols, and ensuring the safety of his president. It was a responsibility he relished, although he'd never admit it. Behind his rugged exterior, he loved being the "Billy Bad Ass" or the "Tough Guy," as I fondly liked to call him.

I recall one memorable ride with our club, a vibrant convoy of twenty to thirty bikes navigating the open road. The sun beat down upon us, and our parched throats yearned for relief. As we pulled into a dive bar, a sense of both excitement and empathy washed over me. I couldn't help but sympathize with the overwhelmed bartenders, their eyes betraying a hint of panic. In anticipation of our arrival, one of the club's wives would often reach out to the establishment, providing an advance warning and estimated time of our arrival. This small gesture granted the bar some reprieve, allowing them to muster extra staff to meet our needs.

One by one, we rumbled into the bar, seeking comfort from the sweltering heat in the cool, air-conditioned haven. Inside, we engaged in lively conversations, relishing the fellowship that came with being part of this tight-knit group. Yet, as fate would have it, a disruptive encounter unfolded before my eyes. A random individual approached the president of our club, his demeanor laden with agitation and discontent. John, ever vigilant and seldom straying far, was by the president's side in an instant. Without hesitation, he swiftly intervened, defusing the escalating tension. With assertive resolve, he escorted the man out of the bar, restoring peace to the scene. Such incidents were rare, but when they arose, John was there, unyielding in his commitment to safeguarding the club's harmony. It was moments like these that solidified his love for his position within the club's ranks.

As I observed John in his role as the sergeant at arms, I admired his unwavering dedication and the sense of purpose it brought to his life. His embodiment of strength and protection served as a testament to the brotherhood he cherished within his motorcycle club. With each passing day, I grew to understand the significance of his role and the deep-rooted ties that bound them together as a united front.

I embraced my time in this season of our life and took pride in being a participant in John's club, even if it was from the sidelines. There was no denying that the club knew how to have a good time, and we certainly had our fair share of fun. While it's true that there was some drinking and occasional use of pot within the club, it never went beyond that. At least nothing that I witnessed. Personally, I wasn't a fan of smoking pot as it didn't sit well with my lungs and left me feeling anxious and paranoid. On a few occasions, I joined my girlfriends in sharing a joint, which always ended with me coughing uncontrollably and nearly gagging, which seemed to really entertain my friends. I was clearly an amateur in that department. Now, when it came to alcohol, that was a different story. I enjoyed it, and if I wanted to endure long rides on the back of John's motorcycle, it became somewhat of a crutch. It allowed me to relax and alleviate my anxiety.

I'll admit, even though the guys in the club were experienced and safe riders, my mind couldn't help but wander to thoughts of deer darting across the road or inattentive drivers. My imagination ran wild. I would become plagued with worrisome scenarios, envisioning nuts and bolts coming loose and the front tire suddenly detaching. I would constantly whisper questions into John's ear, "Is the bike supposed to be making that sound? Are the tires properly inflated?" I'm sure I drove him crazy. My doctor had prescribed Xanax for my headaches, but I found that taking one with a shot of whiskey and Diet Coke before hopping on the back of his bike helped calm my nerves. The problem with this was the combination of fresh air and the cocktail would often lull me to sleep, causing me to inadvertently slump forward and bump my helmet against the back of John's head. It's a wonder I stayed upright at all. As a result, his concerns shifted from listening to my complaints from the backseat to worrying about me toppling off the bike. I certainly wasn't the easiest passenger, and he let me know that on more than one occasion.

I'm grateful to God for watching over us during that phase of our lives, sending His angels to protect us along the way.

During that time, my relationship with God was lukewarm at best. If someone had asked, I would have identified myself as a Catholic, believing it to be the one true religion—the original church. I had always acknowledged God's existence, but I saw no urgency to deepen my faith. I thought I had a sufficient understanding of Him.

However, the words from Revelation 3:15-16 (ESV) echoed a truth that I had failed to recognize: "I know your deeds, that you are neither cold nor hot. I wish you were either one or the other! So, because you are lukewarm— neither hot nor cold—I am about to spit you out of my mouth."

I held a skeptical view of the church, believing it to be filled with hypocrites. My connection with God, if it could even be called that, was found on the back of John's motorcycle. I prayed a lot for our safety. I didn't discuss God or faith because I had no personal relationship with Him. Instead, I entrusted my faith to God's hands, assuming if He loved me and I believed in Him, it would be sufficient to secure my place in Purgatory. I was content with that outcome. I had friends and family within the church who I believed at the time could pray for me or contribute financially to aid my journey from Purgatory to Heaven, eventually. I wholeheartedly embraced the philosophy of living life to the fullest, guided by whatever brought me the most joy. Whether my actions were considered sinful or not held little significance to me. I was determined to seize every opportunity to experience the richness of life.

Chapter Three
Climbing the Ladder

"Pride brings a person low, but the lowly in spirit gain honor." ~ Proverbs 29:23 (NIV)

THE FX SERIES, SONS of Anarchy, reignited America's fascination with the motorcycle world, captivating audiences with its portrayal of old-school outlaws and modern-day cowboy gunslingers. The show was a rollercoaster of drama, featuring intriguing characters and thunderous bikes that echoed through the screen. Its depiction of sex, drugs, and violence fulfilled the cravings of those seeking an adrenaline-fueled TV experience centered on an outlaw motorcycle club.

This surge of interest led to a peculiar phenomenon: people who had never laid a hand on a Harley suddenly felt drawn to the allure of being an outlaw, or at least pretending to be one. Executives splurged on expensive bikes and dressed themselves in full leather gear from head to toe, transforming into weekend warriors. Come Fridays, they would proudly flaunt their unshaven faces, attempting to embody the rugged toughness they admired. However, discerning eyes like John's and mine could spot these individuals from a mile away. They had a nickname among true bikers—Rubs (Rich Urban Bikers). The silver lining, though, was that when they eventually grew tired of their faux outlaw personas, they often sold their bikes with very few miles on them at a great price.

PROPERTY OF THE KING

It's surprising how many people I come across who have no real understanding of what it's like to be part of, or associated with, a motorcycle club. I used to be one of those people until John introduced me to this thrilling new adventure. Little did I know, I was about to embark on a journey of living a double life. With clients or family, I mostly spoke the truth if they inquired, but I seldom shared much about this hidden aspect of my life with anyone.

New riders, as well as family and friends, have a distorted perception of the motorcycle world. They either believe it mirrors the exaggerated portrayal seen on TV, or they dismiss it all as pure fiction.

Before delving further into this book, it is crucial to explain the various levels within the motorcycle world. Within the motorcycle culture, there is a distinct hierarchy of authority and power. As a biker ascends the ranks, they gain greater influence and command within the brotherhood community. Basically, you have four different levels: riding clubs, motorcycle clubs, support clubs, and 1%er (one-percenter) clubs.

There are riding associations or groups that exist within the motorcycle world. These riding clubs operate differently from traditional motorcycle clubs and have a more relaxed and informal structure.

Riding clubs are composed of individuals who share a common passion for riding motorcycles. The primary focus of these clubs is to enjoy group rides and the freedom of the open road. Members come together regularly to embark on rides as a collective, enjoying the camaraderie and shared experiences of riding with fellow bikers.

Riding clubs have fewer commitments and obligations. Members have the freedom to come and go as they please, and there is less emphasis on strict allegiance to the group. These clubs often have a more inclusive and welcoming atmosphere, readily accepting non-members and inviting them to take part in club events and rides.

The patches worn by members of riding clubs typically consist of a one-piece patch, reflecting

the club's name or logo. There is usually little classification or hierarchy among the members, as the focus is more on the enjoyment of riding and the shared experience, rather than formal ranks or positions.

Riding clubs center their activities around social and group-friendly events that embrace the broader motorcycle community. They organize gatherings, rallies, and rides that are open to all riders, fostering a sense of inclusivity and fellowship. The leadership within riding clubs tends to be more flexible and loosely structured, allowing for a greater level of participation and input from members.

Because of their welcoming nature and emphasis on group enjoyment, riding clubs can rapidly grow in size and popularity. They provide an avenue for riders to connect, share their love for motorcycles, and explore the open road together. It was within this type of club that John initially found his place when he moved to the Upper Peninsula of Michigan, immersing himself in the riding community and forging connections with like-minded individuals.

The next level in the motorcycle world is the motorcycle club (MC). Joining a motorcycle club requires a higher level of commitment and dedication compared to a riding club. In a motorcycle club, the members form a close-knit family, and their bond goes beyond their shared love for motorcycles.

PROPERTY OF THE KING

Membership in a motorcycle club entails certain responsibilities and obligations. Dues are required, and regular attendance and active participation in group events and functions are essential. Meetings are exclusive to club members, creating a sense of exclusivity and privacy within the club. Prospects, who are individuals aspiring to become full members, have limited access to meetings and club functions until they earn their full membership status.

What sets a motorcycle club apart is the deep sense of brotherhood among its members. They are not just riding partners but individuals who can be relied upon and trusted in various aspects of life, extending beyond the realm of motorcycles. The members share a special bond and support one another both on and off their bikes.

To establish a motorcycle club, approval is needed from the dominant "1%er club" in the area. These 1%er clubs are recognized as the leading authorities in the motorcycle world and have established territories. Motorcycle clubs typically wear a three-piece patch, signifying their organized structure and membership status. They fall under the territorial jurisdiction of one of the prominent 1%er clubs, known as the "Big Five."

John played a significant role in elevating the riding club he initially joined to the status of a motorcycle club. This transition required effort and commitment from the members, and John was instrumental in making it happen. He remained at this level, actively involved with the motorcycle club for quite some time. However, his adventurous spirit and desire for more power and authority led him to seek further progression within the MC world, eventually leading him to the third level.

The third step in the MC world is becoming a support club for the "1%ers," the dominant MCs in the community. Being a support club means operating under the authority and leadership of a specific 1%er club. Support clubs play a subordinate role to the 1%er club and follow their rules, regulations, and guidance.

In the MC communities, whether affiliated with a club or not, respect is often acquired through fear and intimidation. As individuals progress higher in the bike world, they tend to gain more respect from others. This respect, however, is often based on a false perception and can be rooted in the reputation, power, and authority associated with their position within the hierarchy.

It's important to note that while fear and intimidation may be prevalent in some segments of the MC culture, not all individuals or clubs adhere to such practices. There are many riders and clubs who prioritize camaraderie, mutual respect, and the shared love for motorcycles, rather than relying on fear-based dynamics. Each person's experience and perception of respect may vary within the diverse motorcycle MC community.

The fourth level in the MC world is occupied by the 1%ers, which refers to outlaw motorcycle clubs such as the Hells Angels, Bandidos, Pagans, Mongols, or the Outlaws. The term "1% Motorcycle Club" originated after the 1947 Hollister Riot in Hollister, California. The American Motorcycle Association (AMA) stated that 99% of motorcycle riders are law-abiding citizens, and the 1%ers declared themselves as the remaining 1%. In the late 1940s, after World War II, there was a rise in outlaw motorcycle clubs, as many returning servicemen sought the thrill and camaraderie they experienced during the war.

PROPERTY OF THE KING

These organized motorcycle clubs wear a vest called a "cut" that typically consists of a leather or denim vest adorned with three patches. The top patch, known as the "top rocker," displays the club's name, while the center patch features the club's logo. The bottom patch, referred to as the "bottom rocker," indicates the geographical territory of the club. The 1%ers distinguish themselves with a diamond-shaped back patch, signifying their club status. It's worth noting that most MCs require at least a year of membership before allowing members to tattoo any club patches on their bodies.

While there is a perception of violence associated with 1%er clubs, most club-related violent crimes occur between rival clubs. Generally, the saying "Stay out of their way, and they will stay out of yours." holds true. However, it's important to remember that not all 1%er clubs engage in criminal activities, and there are variations in the behavior and values within the 1%er community.

It is worth mentioning that certain 1%er clubs may have support clubs (level three) associated with them. Support clubs exist because there are certain illicit activities or tasks that even the most feared clubs prefer not to handle directly. In such cases, the support club, like the one John was a part of, is called upon to assist. Support club members often refer to the members of their associated 1%er club as their Big Brothers, highlighting the hierarchical relationship and loyalty within the community.

The support club associated with 1%er organizations is subject to scrutiny and surveillance by law enforcement agencies. John once tried to ease my concerns by saying, "The fact that an organization has members who are criminals does not mean that the entire organization is criminal." He attempted to reassure me, but in hindsight, I wish I had conducted a quick Google search and discover the true nature of these associations.

Both the support clubs and 1%er clubs are highly structured criminal organizations, engaging in activities such as violent crime, weapons trafficking, and drug trafficking. It is essential to understand that these groups operate outside the boundaries of the law. While not all support club members are involved in criminal activities (as John said), the organizations as a whole are associated with illegal practices.

Gaining knowledge about these aspects of the MC world through research would have provided me with valuable insights and a better understanding of the potential risks and implications involved.

In the MC world, when one of the big brothers gave Johnny an order, he didn't question it but knew to act immediately! Failure to comply would result in severe consequences. The level of obedience and respect expected within these clubs was unwavering.

I vividly recall the time when my husband was in the probate phase of joining the support club. As a probate, he held a position at the bottom of the hierarchy. While he wasn't yet a full-fledged member, he still possessed more authority and influence than the MCs beneath him. He had to endure a probationary period, during which he remained discreet and only spoke when spoken to. Club matters were kept strictly confidential, and he familiarized himself with every member's name. He made it a point to be the first to arrive at events and the last to leave. Whenever a fellow member experienced a breakdown, regardless of the time, he offered his help without hesitation. He followed instructions diligently. The process of earning his patches and being fully initiated into the brotherhood, known as getting "patched in," could take anywhere from six months to a year, depending on the club.

As part of his role, he carried an assortment of items in his pockets at all times: condoms, fingernail clippers, Excedrin, Tums, lighters, and even once requested one of my tampons. When I asked why, he nonchalantly replied, "To plug a bullet wound." It was a stark reminder of the darkness that existed within this world. He kept these items readily available in case a 1%er or a fully patched member required them. I'm certain there were other undisclosed objects concealed in his pockets, reserved for club members only, and certainly not shared with me or non-members.

When I recount my experiences in the MC world, it begins with my husband's involvement in the riding club, which eventually led to his transition into the second level. However, most of my story revolves around John's affiliation with the support club of the 1%er club he belonged to. I consider it to be a middle ground within the MC hierarchy. He wasn't at the pinnacle of the MC world, despite being offered opportunities to probate for the 1%er club, nor was he at the bottom.

As a woman in a predominantly male-dominated world, I found myself in a unique position. I wasn't privy to the club's confidential information, but I knew more than I wished to know—it was often more than I could handle. Perhaps I had a better understanding of certain rules than the new probates, but there was no room for a woman's opinions or speculations in these clubs. Women were expected to understand their place, and I was aware of mine, although I didn't always conform to it as successfully as expected.

John's path to becoming a support member for the 1%er club was a gradual and challenging journey. It demanded unwavering commitment, fierce loyalty, and the gradual accumulation of respect from fellow club brothers. In the upcoming chapter, I will delve deeper into the intricate steps and experiences that paved the way for Johnny's entry into this exclusive realm.

Chapter Four

Stepping Up

"Though I walk in the midst of trouble, you preserve my life; you stretch out your hand against the wrath of my enemies, and your right hand delivers me." ~ Psalm 138:7 (ESV)

IN TOMAHAWK, WISCONSIN, AN annual bike rally takes place that draws tens of thousands of bikers. It's truly remarkable how a small town with just over three thousand residents can accommodate such a massive influx of up to forty thousand bikers for an entire weekend. The rally, held in the fall, holds a special significance as it honors and celebrates our veterans while also supporting important causes like the Never Forgotten Honor Flight, Wounded Warriors in Action/Foundation, and organizing VFW blood drives and veteran breakfasts. Tomahawk itself is a charming town often referred to as the "Gateway to the Northwoods." John and I made sure not to book any salon appointments during this time of year.

Given the unpredictable weather conditions, ranging from scorching heat to snow and rain, it was essential to dress appropriately for the ride. In this part of Wisconsin, experiencing a temperature change of forty degrees within a twenty-four-hour period is not uncommon. However, with the right gear and preparation, we embraced the challenge with little concern.

Johnny's motorcycle club had managed to rent out an entire resort for the weekend, and we found ourselves sharing the modest little cabins among us. These cabins were far from luxurious. The showers had perpetually clogged drains, so I'd silently pray each morning to beat my hungover bunk mates to avoid standing in their murky bathwater up to my knees. The mattresses were nothing more than springs, offering little comfort. If you had the pleasure of sharing a bed with someone, it was a constant battle of either rolling together into the center or inevitably finding the lighter person sliding down towards the heavier one. There was no escaping the proximity of your friends at the kitchen table, and like mischievous children, we would giggle at the awkward sounds coming from our intoxicated buddies attempting to make love. I was convinced that the cabin decorations consisted of discarded furniture found on the side of the road. Any notion of resort living standards was abandoned the moment we stepped through the cabin doors.

Fortunately, the resort had a decent bar and restaurant, which was managed by an elderly Russian gentleman. His command of the English language was limited, but he had an impressive talent for mixing potent drinks. He had his own signature concoction, and whenever I was offered a shot, I would politely decline with a tilted head and a wink, knowing that the strength of that drink was far beyond my tolerance.

This place was a paradise for those who reveled in wild parties. The best part was that nobody had to worry about the responsibility of driving home, especially on two wheels. John, known affectionately as "Johnny" by his brothers, wasn't much of a drinker himself. So, we took a ride into town on our own, with Johnny serving as the sober driver. Our friends, not wanting to risk any mishaps, stayed behind to enjoy the company of the Russian owner and revel in the freedom from responsibilities.

STREETS OF TOMAHAWK

The streets of the small town were alive with activity as they blocked the main drag off for the festivities. Everywhere we looked, there was entertainment and an array of food options. After indulging in some people-watching and devouring corn dogs, Johnny and I hopped back on his bike and headed towards a park that had been transformed into a makeshift festival ground. Our experience took an unexpected turn as we were confronted by swarms of black flies. It was rumored that a neighboring resident, unhappy with the influx of bikers, had arranged for cow manure to be spread along the property lines, resulting in the troublesome outbreak of flies.

Navigating through the maze of vendors, offering everything from bike parts, clothing and accessories, to food, beer, and various memorabilia, we encountered a man from a 1%er club who approached us. He was curious about our origins and placed his heavily tattooed forearm around Johnny's neck, steering him away from me for a private conversation. Left standing alone, I felt a wave of intimidation wash over me, triggered by the tattoos on the man's forehead and the members surrounding him resembling a pack of hungry wolves. I couldn't help but wonder what they had in store for my husband. The uncertainty weighed on me, and all I could do was keep my head down and try to remain calm. Time seemed to stretch on indefinitely.

Finally, I spotted Johnny making his way back to me, and a sense of relief flooded over me. "Thank God!" I exclaimed. "I'll just stand here by myself, completely terrified."

Johnny responded, "Deb, I had to go. What else could I do? They want to set up a meeting with the president of our club. They're serious about it."

"For what?" I asked, my nerves still on edge. He never responded directly to my question. Instead, he said, "Let's go check out their vendor booth. I have a feeling we might need a couple of support hoodies and t-shirts from their club."

I remember returning to the resort wearing the sweatshirt I just purchased from the 1%er MC that had approached Johnny. Our friends seemed nervous about me wearing it, warning me it could be dangerous. I was puzzled. Sure, they appeared to be shady-looking characters, but I had worn support swag from other clubs before, just never from a 1%er club. What was the issue? What did they know that I didn't?

Shortly after the eventful gathering in Tomahawk, I noticed our newfound friends from the 1%er MC showing up at parties at John's MC. A few of them would ride into town, including the pack of intimidating individuals I had encountered in Tomahawk. They were treated with the utmost respect and privilege, never having to pay for anything. They commanded attention wherever they went, and people would make way for them as if they were royalty. It was as if they had a special status. And Johnny's MC always dispatched a couple of brothers on their bikes to meet them at the state border, as if they were providing security for the President of the United States.

PROPERTY OF THE KING

Suddenly, the 1%er MC and their support club started making appearances in our town every weekend, arriving in groups of three or four. They never traveled alone, especially when they were proudly displaying their club insignia on their backs. Their presence made people nervous, including myself. They'd shown up at local events before, but never as much as this. So why were they here now? What were their intentions?

Johnny began talking more and more about this support club and gradually sharing bits and pieces of what their world looked like. Looking back, I realized he had likely sugar-coated the realities, but I wasn't sure if he did it for my sake or his own.

The decision to leave his current MC and join the support club, stepping up to a regional 1%er club status, was a significant one. I trusted Johnny to make the right choices, but I couldn't help but feel uncertain. The members of the support club began handpicking individuals from Johnny's club, whom they believed would be a good fit for their ranks. They had their eyes on Johnny, and he started meeting with them regularly. It was the beginning of a new chapter, and I had a feeling it was going to be quite the ride.

Chapter Five

Welcome to a New World

"Be strong and courageous. Do not be afraid or terrified because of them, for the LORD your God goes with you; he will never leave you nor forsake you." ~ Deuteronomy 31:6 (NIV)

When stepping up to the next level of an MC, there's no turning back. Johnny could never go backwards, as he called it, only forward. Once committed, there's no "I changed my mind" clause in the bylaws. It's a decision that demands unwavering dedication. If it turns out that this MC isn't your thing, the only way out is to embrace a new path: either ascending to a bigger, stronger, and superior club by joining the ranks of a 1%er or making the difficult choice to step out of the biker world completely.

Although there was no support club chapter in our area at the time, other chapters of the support club were determined to establish one. This endeavor required significant effort, time, and financial resources to bring to fruition. It also required men willing to step up to the next level and, in doing so, also needed the support and commitment of the women in their lives.

For those men who stepped up, their partners needed to be onboard with the commitment, understanding the demanding nature of this lifestyle. When a man committed to the club, whether it was for a funeral or an event like a national or regional run, he had to go. It didn't matter if Johnny never met the brother that passed. At least two brothers from Johnny's chapter had to be there. This meant leaving behind household responsibilities and work.

The first official meeting aimed at influencing me and other women was orchestrated by Johnny, who believed it would be beneficial for us wives to interact with a woman from another chapter. This woman, referred to as an "old lady" in the MC world, held a significant position within the club's hierarchy and was in a committed relationship with one of its members. The purpose of the meeting was to paint a captivating picture of the biker lifestyle and persuade us to embrace it. And I must admit, she was remarkably effective in her mission. Thus, the grooming of the wives commenced.

Looking back, I now realize the calculated nature of their approach, although at the time, I was oblivious to their intentions. They were skilled at what they did and sent their most influential representative to sway us. One particular old lady had a tough and edgy appearance. Her thin frame, jet-black hair with a hint of purple, and the way she styled it in a rag added to her distinctive look. Tattoos adorned her from her jawline down to her fingertips.

It was impossible not to notice her ample bosom, barely contained within the small piece of fabric she wore beneath her vest. The vest proudly displayed the words "Property of" on the back. I couldn't help but wonder if she was someone's possession, and my imagination wandered. Did she have intimate relationships with all the club members? What was it truly like to wear that cut she had on? My thoughts ran wild. However, she carefully painted a picture of being an old lady, emphasizing the expectations and what was deemed acceptable. Of course, she conveniently omitted the details that would raise concerns for any sensible woman. She assured us that family always came first, followed by career, and then club life—a principle that aligned with the club my husband was leaving.

As she recounted her experiences, one particular story stood out. It was the time when she found herself in a difficult situation, needing to remove her belongings from the house she shared with her abusive ex-husband. Despite the challenges she faced, she discovered a remarkable support system in her life.

She explained that her old man, along with a few other brothers from the MC, not only stood by her side but also ensured her safety and well-being. They protected her while she packed her belongings, ensuring her ex-husband couldn't harm her during the process.

What was even more astonishing was that they went beyond merely offering protection. They took it upon themselves to move her belongings from one state to another.

We were captivated, perched on the edge of our stools, yearning for more insights into life within the biker world. We became hooked on the allure of having the protection and support of an entire organization behind us. She conveyed that in this world, problems with other women from different clubs simply vanished. No woman would dare disrespect you when you had a husband affiliated with a support club. Having my husband involved in such a club would command respect from other bikers, or at the very least, compel them to feign it. It was the first time I experienced that "Billy Badass" feeling for myself. The whole concept was intriguing, mystical, exciting, adventurous and scandalous. Just the thought of being associated with something notorious and renowned worldwide sent adrenaline coursing through my veins. According to her, there was a sense of satisfaction in being respected or feared by ordinary citizens.

PROPERTY OF THE KING

This meeting left me with an insatiable craving to learn more and solidified my unwavering support for my husband's new adventure and decision to become a part of this MC.

I don't recall my husband ever uttering the words, "Let me think about it and discuss it with my old lady to see what she thinks." He was fully committed, without hesitation or reservation. They presented us with an enticing proposition, and I wanted to stand by my husband in this new venture. Despite the fear and uncertainty, it felt like the right thing to do. Johnny had always supported me and my choices in life, whether it was pursuing my dreams of opening a boutique, participating in ultra-marathons, or becoming a photographer. He never said no or discouraged me from following my passions. It was only fair that I reciprocate that same kind of support. I couldn't bring myself to say no, and honestly, I didn't want to.

From an outsider's perspective, being referred to as "property" by an MC may sound derogatory. However, within the biker culture, they make you believe it's a badge of honor. Roxy, the old lady I met, convinced me that the common misconception about being called "property" implied being owned by the entire club and existing solely to serve them was untrue. According to her and the club's narrative, it held a different meaning. Little did I know that this was far from a misconception. Wearing the vest with patches that said "Property of" meant you were indeed owned by the club. While I had no intention of engaging in any form of sexual servitude for the men in the club (that was out of the question), there were other obligations and expectations placed upon me I'd never imagined.

DEBORAH MCKINZIE

THE "PROPERTY OF" PATCH

When the time was deemed right, Johnny would ask me to wear his "Property of" patch. I imagined it feeling like the moment he proposed to me. I was very much looking forward to this moment. I was informed that by accepting this gift, I would be publicly declaring to the entire MC, as well as outsiders, that I was his woman and under his and the club's protection. It was explained to me that the patch also served as a warning to others, signaling that I was taken and should be treated with respect, and that advances or unwanted attention from other members should be avoided. Despite previously believing that my wedding ring conveyed all these messages, I came to understand that in this world, it wasn't enough. The club demanded a visible symbol, a clear sign of ownership. Only later did I come to realize that wearing that "Property of" patch carried far deeper implications than what Roxy had initially described.

I found myself spending a significant amount of time with women who, on the surface, seemed quite different from me. Despite our differences, I knew it was crucial to maintain positive relationships with them. It was important to remember that I was an invited guest in my husband's world. If conflicts arose between me and other old ladies, it had the potential to disrupt club events, which would ultimately impact Johnny and his standing within the club.

In this lifestyle, I had no say or control over where we socialized or the activities we engaged in. The men dictated our meeting places, often opting for strip clubs and dive bars when we weren't at the clubhouse. It became increasingly clear that, as an old lady, I was considered a second-class citizen in this male-dominated environment. I had to project an outward appearance of submission and develop a thick skin to endure the frequent sexist remarks or comments. I understood that my club affiliation, including any patches, clothing, and even certain items of jewelry, were all on loan to me by my husband. He had the authority to take them away if he chose to do so.

I spent a lot of time with women that I didn't have a lot in common with. But I had to get along with them. Remember, you are an invited guest. If I caused problems with other old ladies, it's a possibility that I could be blocked from club events, which would have a big impact on Johnny.

What I failed to comprehend then, but would soon come to understand, is that our ultimate protection comes from God. In moments of physical and spiritual assault, and in the face of various threats, those who place their trust in the Lord discover His unwavering role as a mighty Protector. As it is written, "He shields all who take refuge in Him" (Psalm 18:30 NIV).

Reflecting, had I known and acknowledged my ultimate Protector, none of these experiences would have unfolded. I was unaware of the profound lessons I needed to learn through it all. I often questioned why God allowed these circumstances to occur in my life. Why hadn't He revealed Himself to me? What I failed to recognize was that He had been present all along, repeatedly making His presence known. My eyes were blinded, and my ears were deaf to His guidance. I simply wasn't prepared to receive His truth. Yet, despite my lack of awareness, God never departed from my side, nor did He abandon me. He remained steadfast throughout it all.

Chapter Six

Seen Not Heard

"She opens her mouth with wisdom, and the teaching of kindness is on her tongue." ~ Proverbs 31:26 (ESV)

It was in the 15th century that a clergyman named John Mirk first coined the phrase "Children should be seen, but not heard." Unfortunately, this mentality allowed certain adults to wield their power over children and potentially abuse it. As a child, I vividly remember being told repeatedly to sit still and keep my mouth shut, thanks to my seemingly endless supply of energy. Little did I know that this mantra of "Be seen and not heard" would continue to influence my life as an adult woman, particularly within the realm of a men's MC.

One distinct moment stands out in my memory when this phrase came back to me in a different form by one of my husband's brothers. "Debbie, don't disrespect your old man in front of other club members," he admonished. In response, I couldn't help but roll my eyes and retort, "Yeah, okay. Please!" I swiftly turned on my heels and walked away, refusing to accept the idea that I should suppress my thoughts and opinions.

In my view, respect is something that must be earned. If my partner was disrespecting me, I firmly believed it was my duty to let him know, no matter who was in the room. The same principle applied to anyone else who showed me disrespect. It didn't take long for me to grasp the significance of the unwritten rule: "Don't disrespect your old man in front of other club members" — a credo that held significant weight among club members themselves.

The anticipation was mounting as the first bar night approached at the newly established clubhouse. We, the members and old ladies, had dedicated countless hours transforming a run-down, two-bedroom rental property into a bona fide biker's paradise. We succeeded.

Day in and day out, we toiled, converting the living room and dining room on the first floor into a sprawling bar area. The centerpiece was a magnificent countertop crafted from giant white pine slabs. It was a sight to behold. We stocked the bar with everything the MC needed.

The club never allowed customers to place their cash directly on the bar for a drink. To avoid potential legal issues, in case an undercover individual appeared, we operated as a private club sustained by donations.

We converted one bathroom into two: His and Hers, although club members were free to use either. As old ladies, we were prohibited from transforming the girls' room into a space of beauty. The idea of placing a fresh vase of flowers on the vanity or leaving a few feminine products in the drawer was simply out of the question. However, I stashed some hairspray and other feminine essentials under the sink for any women in need.

The kitchen remained largely untouched, except for the exhausting task of cleaning up the remnants of mouse infestation that had plagued the cabinets and drawers. The place was truly appalling, making it hard to fathom how anyone could've rented it before the MC moved in.

The main floor, with its inviting bar, became the heart of the clubhouse on bar nights, open to all members and guests. The second floor, however, held an air of exclusivity, reserved solely for club members. This was clearly indicated by a bold sign positioned at the bottom of the stairs leading upstairs.

Within the two bedrooms on the second floor, club members had constructed bunks to accommodate traveling members from other regions. The house could hold up to 15 men, although sleep seemed to elude most of them. While I attempted to furnish the beds with fresh linens and sleeping bags when the clubhouse initially opened, I couldn't help but feel sympathy for the women who ventured upstairs with a brother in tow for a night's stay (whether it lasted an hour or mere minutes, depending on the brother's preference or endurance). One can only imagine the activities and bodily fluids left behind before the next woman ascended those stairs. It was undoubtedly repulsive, yet somehow still a step up from the revolting conditions in some other MC houses I had encountered.

The basement, too, claimed a considerable amount of my time as I meticulously painted its walls. We used gallons upon gallons of paint, ensuring the colors were just right. Colors held significant meaning within the MC culture, serving as a visual representation of a club's identity. These colors were sacred to the club and its members. They served as a means of identification and loyalty, symbolizing the rejection of societal norms and values. The colors embodied pride and camaraderie, connecting members through their shared experiences within the tight-knit MC.

Access to the basement was strictly limited to the MC brothers. It was the space where "church" was held, a term used to describe club meetings. The only exception for women to enter the basement was when an old lady was summoned to clean up the aftermath of disciplinary actions, such as sweeping up the drywall debris left behind after a member had been forcefully thrown into a wall.

I distinctly recall one night when a probate was finally "patched in." This moment marked the culmination of six months of tireless dedication and enduring the belittlement and harassment from other members. The probate could now proudly wear the club patches on his "cut." The brothers would test his resolve by attempting to snatch the cut from his back, and the probate had to fight tooth and nail to keep it. The MC's cut held immense significance. It was never to be left unattended, with brothers even sleeping while wearing their cuts to safeguard against potential raids, where their cuts could be seized as they slept. I recall another instance when a member was thrown into a wall, his right eye swollen shut from the brutal beating he endured, because he fell asleep while guarding the back gate of the clubhouse. The beating was to teach him a lesson.

The basement had only one exit — a door at the top of the stairs, perpetually guarded by a member. It was effectively locked down, ensuring the sanctity of the space within.

Johnny warned me to be on my best behavior one night, adhering to the unspoken rule of being seen and not heard. It was a significant occasion, as I would meet numerous club members from different chapters. Excitement filled the air as I arrived early, ready for my first real immersion into the club life. I had heard tales of the various parties and even attended a few in other states, but this was different. I was eager to witness the pride my husband and his "brothers" took in showcasing their hard work on the new clubhouse.

DEBORAH MCKINZIE

Throughout the night, I took on various tasks to contribute to the event. I diligently kept the bathrooms clean, served food, and attended to minor details like emptying ashtrays and picking up empty beer cans. However, there was an unspoken division of responsibilities, and handling the garbage was strictly designated as a probate's duty, not an old lady's responsibility.

I remember a friend from outside the club questioning why I put in so much effort for these guys. She felt it was disrespectful that I was expected to contribute so much when I didn't receive the same level of respect from the club members. In response, I explained that just as I would go the extra mile to ensure our guests were well taken care of when my husband hosted a party at our own house; I felt the same way about the clubhouse. It was yet another way of supporting Johnny and being a part of his world, even if it meant taking on tasks that might not be recognized or appreciated by everyone in the club.

HOW DARE THEY

Sometime in the early morning, my husband oh-so-politely "asked" if I could do him the immense favor of putting the food away. Because, you know, who needs nourishment when there's excessive drinking involved? But being the nurturing motherly figure that I am, I thought these fine gentlemen could use a little sustenance in their bellies. Guess my husband didn't catch on to my subtle hint, so he asked again. "Could you put the food away?" I tried to muster up my best reply, "I don't think it's a good idea," and started to explain why, as if my opinion mattered in this testosterone-fueled realm.

PROPERTY OF THE KING

Lo and behold, in that glorious moment, a brother from a different chapter swooped in to enlighten my dear husband about the dire consequences of not keeping his old lady in check. Because we all know, the world would end if the boss were to be upset. Who knew my voice carried such weight? I should audition for a megaphone commercial.

Naturally, I was thrilled by the turn of events and promptly grabbed the roaster filled with the remnants of dried-up spaghetti and chicken. With grace and elegance, I made my way to the kitchen, stomping past the bar area where one of the bosses, clearly a master of charm, graced me with his poetic words. "Hey, cunt, get off your ass and pick this place up." Ah, the sweet melodies of endearment.

As I stood there, contemplating my existence, I entertained a vivid mental image of unleashing my inner ninja and using my well-honed black belt skills to teach that individual a lesson in manners. But alas, I quickly snapped back to reality because, you know, consequences and stuff. I couldn't let my impulsive actions jeopardize my husband's status in this esteemed MC. Who knew what kind of punishment awaited him?

Tears streamed down my face as I retreated to the kitchen, like a wounded gazelle running from a bloodbath. Placing the roaster on the counter, I decided to make a grand exit through the back door. But I was reminded that only an MC member can touch the doors. I looked the dude in the eyes without saying a word. He pushed it open for my exit, bathed in moonlight and tinged with a hint of audacity. Perhaps my wedged Nike high-tops weren't the most suitable choice to run home in, but who needs comfort and practicality when escaping from a gathering of intellectual giants?

Of course, my grand escape couldn't be complete without avoiding the watchful eyes of the diligent state police officers patrolling the area. Imagine their confusion if they dared to approach me and inquire about my well-being. "Oh, officer, you see, my feelings were hurt. Can't you tell?" I'm sure they would've been deeply moved by my emotional turmoil.

Inevitably, news of my disappearance reached my husband, and I can only imagine the panic that ensued. He must have feared the wrath of my fiery tongue when he eventually returned home. Did he take a fleeting moment to envision my superhero-like entrance, soaring over the bar and delivering a face-grabbing wake-up call? Oh, the things that must have gone through his mind.

But fear not, for my knight in shining armor, or rather, Johnny's Enforcer, was dispatched to locate me. It took some time, but he eventually caught up with my determined self, huffing and puffing, emitting steam in the frosty midnight air. I was on a mission to find my way home, no matter the odds. And there he was, rolling down the window, offering me the chance of a lifetime—getting a ride home in his truck. How could I refuse such a tempting offer?

SAY YOU'RE SORRY

Ah, yes, the joys of being a woman in the MC world. The phone call from the boss, oh how thoughtful of him. Apologies? Who needs 'em? Especially when it comes to a woman like me, right? It's not like I deserve any basic decency or respect. But hey, at least he appreciated my hard work, because that's all that matters, right? Who needs apologies when you have appreciation?

Oh, and here comes the clarification that the boss wasn't even talking to me in the first place. Silly me, getting all worked up over nothing. I should've known it was just a friendly exchange with those "Property of" ladies sitting behind me. Because, you know, it's totally acceptable to throw around vulgar words and demean women based on their affiliation. It's a real "aha moment" to know that I wasn't the primary target of such charming language. How comforting.

But hey, I'll just keep reminding myself of the age-old mantra: "Be seen, and not heard." Because clearly, my thoughts and feelings have no place in this world. Who needs self-expression or asserting oneself when you can just swallow it all down and pretend everything is fine? I'm just so gifted at keeping my inner turmoil under wraps. Really, I should win an award for my exceptional talent.

But you know what? Screw that. I've never been good at playing by those ridiculous rules. I'm not about to muzzle myself and hide my thoughts and feelings. It's time to break free from this suffocating expectation and let my voice be heard. So, buckle up, world, because this woman is about to make some noise.

Chapter Seven

Accelerating Bonds

"Have I not commanded you? Be strong and courageous. Do not be frightened, and do not be dismayed, for the LORD your God is with you wherever you go." ~ Joshua 1:9 (ESV)

THERE'S AN INDESCRIBABLE THRILL that comes with sitting on the back of a bike, cruising at a blazing speed of ninety miles per hour. But what amplifies that exhilaration even further is when you're surrounded by twenty to thirty fellow riders, all charging ahead together. It's a mix of anxiety and adrenaline that courses through your veins simultaneously.

For Johnny, his brothers, and their extended club family, this was the essence of riding. They rode so closely they could easily extend a hand to exchange a cigarette or a lighter without missing a beat. Riding motorcycles is far from effortless; it demands constant coordination of your hands and feet. Your focus is solely on the road and the riders surrounding you. Your right hand controls the throttle and front brake, while your left hand operates the clutch and turn signals. Your right foot manages the rear brake, while your left foot shifts the gears up and down. It's a delicate balance that requires skill and concentration beyond what meets the eye.

Motorcycles possess an acceleration that surpasses most cars. With just a twist of the throttle, the world around you transforms instantaneously. Reaching a hundred miles per hour on a bike is a completely different experience than inside a car—it feels doubly intense. There is a profound respect and admiration for the raw power that lies beneath you, a machine that demands both caution and appreciation.

When riding alongside your club, another level of respect is present—the trust in your brothers' riding abilities. It's an unspoken pact. To even have a chance of riding with the club, you must be a proficient rider in your own right. It's a prerequisite, non-negotiable. Riding in such proximity means that if one bike were to go down, the domino effect would likely take them all down. Every decision made while riding carries weight. No one desires the burden of being responsible for a crash, jeopardizing the bikes, or endangering the lives of fellow riders. It's a constant vigilance, a shared responsibility that binds the riders together.

In this world of roaring engines and fierce brotherhood, riding represents unity, trust, and the unbridled power pulsating through each member.

From an aerial perspective, I imagine it would appear like two sinuous black serpents winding their way along the asphalt, slithering through backcountry roads and bustling freeways. It was a sight that never quite put me at ease, but as I've mentioned before, the combination of booze and Xannies helped numb my unease.

The club preferred to ride independently, rarely welcoming unfamiliar riders into their ranks. Occasionally, you'd spot a couple of other MCs riding among them, but they would always remain at the rear of the pack. If anything were to go awry, they would bear the consequences themselves. It was a matter of trust, but it also came down to respect, once again emphasizing the pecking order. The 1%ers led the way, with the support club trailing behind them, followed by other MCs and solitary riders (if permitted) bringing up the rear.

When Johnny initially joined the MC, I didn't have my own bike. Even if I did, I could never ride with the MC. Women were prohibited from riding with MC members. If a woman wished to ride her own bike, she had to maintain a distance of at least a mile or two behind the pack of brothers. If she had a "Property of" cut on, she couldn't wear it while riding her bike. I never encountered a woman in the club who desired to ride independently; they were far from being advocates of feminism.

Helmets were not commonplace among riders, unless mandated by state law. My husband's helmet sported a counterfeit sticker claiming its compliance with the Department of Transportation (DOT) regulations, although it was far from legitimate. "Wearing a fake helmet while riding a bike is akin to combating a fire with a counterfeit extinguisher." Of course, I refrained from voicing this sentiment to him.

I, on the other hand, almost always wore my helmet. While it may not have guaranteed my safety at the breakneck speeds we reached, I never wanted my father to ask the dreaded question, "Was she wearing a helmet?" and receive the disheartening response of "No." If an accident were to occur, I wanted him to know that I had taken the precaution of wearing my helmet. It provided him with a bit of peace, however small it may be.

Because of our geographical location, we were blessed with a mere six months of riding season. However, that didn't grant anyone an "acceptable" excuse to arrive at a club event with anything other than a bike. With chapters scattered throughout the United States, if the club called for your presence, you showed up astride your motorcycle. Cars were not an option. It didn't matter how frigid the air was; as long as the road was free of ice, and weather permitted, you rode your bike. Even if your bike was a rat bike, barely held together and maintained just enough to keep it rolling, appearances were of little concern.

I overheard Johnny bellowing into the phone, "Take a pill and ride your damn bike!" Curious, I inquired, "What's going on?" "Rocket isn't taking his bike again! He's opting for his car instead, citing yet another migraine," Johnny grumbled. "What's the big deal?" I asked. Having endured migraines throughout my entire life, I empathized with Rocket's pain.

"The big deal is that I'll get chewed out when Tank, the boss of the 1%ers, asks why he's not on his bike again!" Johnny retorted with frustration. "Nan-na poo-poo can't ride? If he feels well enough to be at a party, then he should ride his damn bike. We're a motorcycle club, not a damn car club. You better sort this out pronto," Tank bellowed through the phone. My old man never put his brothers or big brothers on speakerphone, but I could hear Tank's voice as if he were in the room with us, and it sent shivers down my spine.

The last encounter I had with Tank took place at a 1%ers clubhouse in a state far from home. The ATF had the clubhouse completely surrounded, ATF being the Bureau of Alcohol, Tobacco, Firearms, and Explosives—an American law enforcement agency. The club was under lockdown; no one could enter or leave. They were itching to apprehend us all. Tank glanced at me and casually ordered me, "Darlin', fetch me a tall glass of milk." Internally, I was panicking. Forget about the countless questions swirling in my mind about our fate, the prospect of sleeping on those lovely mattresses, or the urgent need for bail money. How long would we be confined within these walls? And amidst it all, Tank's calm request for a large glass of milk seemed insane and left me dumbfounded.

Tank had a lovely collection of facial tattoos, making him the epitome of approachable and cuddly. (Ha!) He also stood at an astonishing 6'5" and had a weight that could rival a giant. And let's not forget his esteemed position within the club, a position that demanded utmost reverence. When Tank opened his mouth, it was as if the heavens themselves were speaking, and we mere mortals had no choice but to listen in awe. So naturally, I obediently fulfilled his beverage request, scurrying off to fetch him a glass of milk. Oh, how I couldn't resist adding a touch of sarcasm to the mix, flashing a sly smile and gritting my teeth as I asked, "No cookies with that, sir?" Because, you know, a glass of milk is never complete without a side of delicious cookies. Even if the possibility of going to jail is around the corner.

TRAVELING AND LOCATION

You always had a brother by your side when you wore your cut. Riding alone was frowned upon. Fortunately, our area was home to only one 1%er club, so the worry of encountering rival clubs was minimal. If there had been more clubs around, it would have surely been a bigger concern.

I can recall a particular incident when my husband and a few brothers had to leave a party hastily to meet a rival club passing through our town en route to a neighboring state. Prior to their arrival, a phone call was made to one of the bosses, notifying them of the impending visit. The rival club members had to remove their cuts or wear them inside out as a sign of respect while passing through Johnny's MC territory.

In a show of courtesy, my husband's chapter would escort them, ensuring their safe passage and only allowing brief stops for gas along the way. They extended this gesture of respect to all clubs, creating an unspoken code of conduct.

Location was also a critical factor for us. Whenever I was with the club, I was strictly forbidden from having the location feature on my iPhone turned on. It had to be turned off at all times. Curiosity got the better of me, and I wondered how they could possibly know if it was on. Well, I soon discovered their methods. I had been working diligently on building my personal brand through social media, as I had been attempting to Kickstart a small business selling makeup with multi-level marketing. I had a sizable following who avidly watched my videos and selfies. To make the algorithm work in my favor, I needed to post frequently throughout the day. The more I posted, the more exposure my posts received, and the greater the chances of receiving comments, likes, and love reactions. It was a numbers game, and I needed as many people as possible engaging with my content to bolster my makeup sales and establish my empire, albeit a modest one. Posting was non-negotiable—it was my ticket to potential success.

As I juggled the demands of the club and my entrepreneurial aspirations, I realized that finding the delicate balance between loyalty and personal ambition would be a formidable challenge. Little did I know my journey had only just begun.

We had embarked on a multi-day excursion with the club when an irate brother brought a concerning matter to our attention. Someone had taken it upon themselves to play the role of a GPS tracker and informed us of their newfound skill.

"How did they know?" questioned Johnny, though deep down, he had a pretty good hunch. He had an inkling about what had gone awry.

"Well, Debbie, it seems your iPhone had its location turned on, and every picture you posted on Facebook and Instagram kindly divulged our exact whereabouts," I admitted, my tone laced with a sarcastic touch. Oops, my bad. It was a mistake I vowed never to repeat.

"SOCIAL MEDIA SLIP-UPS"

Now, let me clarify something—I was well aware that posting a picture of someone in their cut was an absolute no-go. It was a cardinal rule that should never be broken. NEVER! But alas, some random women at the bar had a peculiar fascination with club brothers. Intoxicated and often star-struck, they would boldly approach these rough-around-the-edges guys and insist on capturing the moment for eternity on their social media accounts. Oh, the allure of the enigmatic bad-boy biker had its hold on these ladies, just as it had for me at the beginning of this journey. Perhaps they wanted to showcase their wild side or give their online persona a touch of naughtiness. They were always sternly instructed not to reveal the club members' patches when posting their precious selfies. Trust me when I say this was an enormous pain in my butt. I found myself in countless situations where I had to approach complete strangers, my polite smile masking the underlying annoyance, and request that they promptly delete any photos they had taken. "Hello there, you don't know me, but I couldn't help but notice you just snapped a picture of a couple of my friends. It would be greatly appreciated if you could delete those," I would diplomatically implore.

Oh, the joys of being the unofficial social media police for the club. Little did I know that navigating the treacherous waters of technology and secrecy would become an integral part of my journey alongside the club.

Usually, with a sassy remark back, these defiant individuals would respond with a challenging, "Why? What are you going to do about it?" Ah, the audacity! At that moment, I would instinctively cast a discreet side glance toward the Enforcer. My look conveyed a silent message. "I'm doing my best here. She's being difficult and refuses to delete the picture. She has no clue what she's getting herself into." I silently muttered to myself, feeling a mix of exasperation and amusement. It often took just a few intimidating glances from these formidable men to make it abundantly clear to these women that I meant business, and they promptly complied, deleting the picture.

What I was really trying to do was save their precious phones from potential trouble. Show me you've deleted it, and we can all move on smoothly. You can keep your precious iPhone, and I can resume my rightful place on the barstool, thoroughly enjoying my evening. Thank you very much.

In the end, it was a delicate dance of asserting authority while maintaining a sense of diplomacy. It was a role I never asked for, but one that I had to assume to protect the club and its members, even if it meant playing the role of the unofficial phone-saving hero.

Although my iPhone couldn't have its location turned on, the club always wanted to keep tabs on Johnny's whereabouts. Even if we wanted to have a little getaway on our own, Johnny had to inform his brothers. The chapter's boss in the city we were visiting would expect Johnny to make an appearance at some point. It could be quite bothersome. I mean, we were adults, capable of making our own decisions. Heck, even my own family didn't know where I was most of the time. But in this new family of mine, they insisted on knowing our location, citing it was for our own safety. They claimed they would be there for us if any problems arose. I never quite grasped what problems they were referring to. If I ever had an issue, I simply called my dad.

Living life in the fast lane went far beyond the club's need for speed. It meant immersing ourselves in a world filled with danger, where the extraordinary became ordinary, and excitement thrived on risky behavior.

Both Johnny and I found ourselves living under a certain level of control. I carefully measured my words, made sure not to indulge in too much alcohol, and remained aware of the places I could or couldn't go. I even paid attention to the colors I wore, lest they be interpreted as a sign of disrespect or allegiance to the wrong crowd. Johnny, despite being a boss himself, was still beholden to his own boss. He had to walk the walk and play his part.

It's strange how quickly we adapted to this kind of control. It became our new normal.

Chapter Eight

Unexpected Conversations

"Then the Lord God said, 'It is not good that the man should be alone; I will make him a helper fit for him.'" ~ Genesis 2:18 ESV

THE ROLE OF BEING an "old lady" in the MC changed over the years while my husband was involved with the MC. During the first six months that Johnny was probating for the support club, it was rare that I would be invited to go anywhere. As a probate, he worked at all club functions. There was little to no time to entertain me or make sure I was okay. His focus was on keeping his brothers happy. If I was fortunate enough to accompany him to club events or parties, I mostly stayed quiet. I would stand by his side or linger in the background while he conversed with his brothers. I didn't say much because I didn't know anyone, and forging friendships in that environment was far from easy.

If there were other women present, I would attempt to spend time with them, but I felt intimidated. They didn't exactly extend a warm invitation, and being new to the biker world, I struggled to earn their trust. I didn't want to say anything wrong and unintentionally offend someone. I longed to be included in the conversations and enjoyment.

As for my appearance, I typically dressed in biker attire: snug, ripped jeans, black leather boots, and support shirts or sweatshirts.

Support shirts bear the words "I support" followed by the MC's name. Some of these shirts carried explicit messages, while others simply displayed the club's name and logo. Wearing them allowed me to feel connected to the club and signify my association with Johnny.

Being together with my old man and his brothers in the MC was an intimidating experience. I'd observe people swiftly moving to the other side of a restaurant when Johnny's MC entered, clutching their children protectively. This always saddened me deeply because I would willingly shield any child from harm. I also noticed others shaking their heads disapprovingly.

When my old man's chapter first opened, and he was finally patched in, I'd ride to the clubhouse with other old ladies for an open bar night. These were the evenings when the public or friends of the MC brothers could stop in and enjoy a drink. Open bar nights usually took place during the week and didn't attract many outsiders. It was a laid-back, and honestly, somewhat dull affair. To pass the time, I started crafting bracelets out of beads. The spacious bar area provided an excellent workspace for me. I know it might seem unusual to envision me engaging in arts and crafts at the clubhouse, as movies and documentaries tend to depict club life as a wild, smoke-filled, and noisy environment. However, it wasn't always like that, and I was perfectly content with that. I made jewelry specifically for the club to sell. I incorporated the MC's initials or colors into the designs, allowing them to be sold alongside the club's merchandise.

Engaging in jewelry making helped me cope with my ADD. My mind is constantly in overdrive, and it doesn't shut off easily. So, when I have the opportunity to slow down, whether that is at a bar or watching TV, I often become lethargic. The clubhouse was perpetually dimly lit and filled with cigarette smoke, which made almost anyone feel tired. The loud, head-banging music they played had the opposite effect on me. Nevertheless, I could sleep through it easily. There were no fans to circulate the stagnant air, and the windows were drywalled over, so it wasn't like you could open them to get fresh air. Club members couldn't care less if you could cut the air with a knife; that was your problem. They would tell me to quit being a little bitch.

The clubhouse doors were always locked. Apparently, there was concern about outsiders, or as they referred to them, civilians, seeing what was happening inside. MC members also had to worry about the state police often driving by, trying to sneak a peek or two inside the clubhouse.

If I didn't keep myself busy, I would doze off on the couch. I'm sure sometimes people who didn't know me must have assumed I was drunk and passed out. But the truth was just the opposite, in fact. I was usually sober, bored, and exhausted, and my eyes were on fire from the smoke, causing them to be bloodshot and swollen. Yet, I didn't want to go home for fear of missing out on something. Sounds exciting, right?

Johnny would wake me up when it was time to leave or if a 1%er walked in. It would have been considered rude if they caught me sleeping on the couch.

On bar nights, Johnny's club consisted of just a few of us, creating an intimate and familiar atmosphere. However, when the weekends rolled around, everything shifted gears. Waves of brothers and their devoted old ladies descended upon us from various states, transforming the scene into a pulsating hub of energy and excitement. The once tranquil bar now brimmed with life as the air crackled with anticipation. It became a magnet for those seeking a taste of the wild side, reaching capacity and overflowing with revelers who embraced the spirit of rock stars. Weekends turned into a vivid kaleidoscope of sights and sounds, a whirlwind of shared moments and unforgettable experiences.

When Johnny's chapter finally opened, the original club he was a part of was furious. They held a grudge for a long time when he left and refused to support the chapter he had joined. They didn't want to show up, but they were obligated to make occasional appearances to maintain good standing with the top dogs of the MC world, the 1%ers.

Things became even more interesting when we ventured beyond Johnny's clubhouse and visited other MCs. In our area, there are six different MCs, all affiliated with the same 1%er MC. Each club took turns hosting parties at their clubhouse on weekends. Most of these clubs were a couple of hours away from each other, turning it into an all-day event. We would embark on a thrilling ride, followed by a massive party. We would fill our bellies with the endless amount of food the old ladies had prepared, and we would enjoy each other's company. One of my favorite aspects of the parties was witnessing the various games they held. There was the Keg Roll, where a biker had to push a keg of beer with the front tire of his bike to the other side of the field without putting his feet on the ground or tipping the bike over. This was an extremely difficult thing to do, considering how slow the bike was going. The first keg to cross the finish line won.

Another beloved game was the "wiener ride". A hotdog was tied to a string hanging from a clothesline, and the biker would ride under it while the person on the back, usually a woman (but not always), attempted to grab it with her mouth. No hands were allowed. Whoever successfully swallowed the wiener won.

Through these travels, I met many women from the different clubs, and we became friends both within and outside the club.

When my husband moved up to a higher level in the MC, women from the previous riding club he was in worried about me. They would pull me aside whenever they had the chance, their faces filled with concern. I didn't know exactly what they were thinking, but it always bothered me. Did they believe I would be pushed around or mistreated? Did they think it would be like the biker shows they watched on Netflix? I would assure them that everything was great because it mostly was then. Apart from the incident where the boss called me something incredibly disheartening, everything seemed fine. Just fine.

One of my girlfriends from the riding club asked if I was going to wear a "PO" (Property of) vest. I responded affirmatively. To me, it was an honor and privilege to wear it. However, she didn't seem to grasp the significance of the patch. I wanted to explain it to her, just as Roxy had explained it to me, but she wasn't interested. Dismissing me with a wave of her hand, she walked away. I found her reaction rude and disappointing. Later, I recounted the conversation to my husband, hoping for some understanding. However, he simply replied, "She doesn't get it, Deb. Don't try to explain it." At that moment, I realized I hadn't comprehended everything that came with wearing the patch myself. How could I expect her to understand if I didn't fully understand it myself?

One time, Johnny and I were on vacation in Florida, while he was still in the prospecting phase before being officially patched into the MC. He was invited to a party at the chapter's clubhouse. They also extended the invite to include me. He was excited to spend time with his brothers from the Florida chapter, but I was anxious. This clubhouse was shared with the "Big Brothers" of the 1%er club, and it was my first time being in a 1%er clubhouse, unlike the support clubhouses I was accustomed to.

Johnny received a phone call informing us that a group of brothers was waiting for us at a nearby gas station. They would ride with us to the clubhouse, and punctuality was emphasized. (Side note: Johnny was always late for everything, except for tee times or appointments with 1%ers!)

"Deb, are you ready? Come on! We have to get going," Johnny exclaimed in an irritated voice. "I'm braiding my hair. Give me a sec. These damn extensions make my head so much bigger that wearing a helmet hurts. Should I wear it?" I replied, seeking his opinion. "Do whatever you want, Deb."

With a confident smirk on my face, I declared, "Let's go." I stole one last glance in the mirror, ensuring that I flawlessly tied my bandana around my head. It hugged my forehead, allowing my expressive eyebrows to add a touch of rebellious charm. I aimed to embody the image of a fierce biker chick, fully immersing myself in the role. My fingers, wrist, and neck were adorned with an abundance of accessories, enough to set off a metal detector from a mile away. My jeans, ripped and distressed, exuded an air of nonchalant coolness. Clad entirely in black, I embraced the club's signature color, with delicate lace teasingly peeking out from under my snug tank top. Even my nails proudly displayed a coat of jet-black polish, while my favorite shade of lipstick had to be set aside. With every element carefully orchestrated, I was ready to embrace the allure and mystique of the biker lifestyle.

Johnny gave me a quick pep talk before we headed out the door, knowing that this experience was not new to him. He wanted to ensure my comfort while emphasizing the importance of good behavior. "Just take it all in, Deb. You don't have to make friends with everyone you meet," he advised.

He knew about my tendency to touch people when I meet them, whether it's a handshake, a hug, or a playful punch on the shoulder. I'm not sure if it's a Midwest thing, a habit from being a hairdresser, or just my own quirk, but physical contact has always been my way of connecting with others. Johnny probably wanted to tell me to be seen and not heard, but he understood better than to make me mad before we left.

The day was perfect for a ride, as one would expect in Florida. We had escaped the harsh winter of Michigan's Upper Peninsula to enjoy the freedom of the open road. For Johnny, the hardest part of living in the UP was having to store his motorcycle for six months of the year because of the unforgiving weather.

When we arrived at the gas station at the appointed time, there were already about 10 bikes waiting. Johnny dismounted his bike and engaged in the familiar fist bump, half-hug ritual with the brothers, while I observed from the sidelines. As we waited for the others to join us, I took in the scene with nervous anticipation. Some old ladies were engaged in a heated conversation, their voices rising. On the other side, a woman stood alone by a bike, drawing the attention of one brother who shouted into his phone, "She shouldn't be here; Taz broke it off with her." Curiosity piqued, I looked on as the other women approached her, bombarding her with questions. I remained silent, hands in my pockets, attempting not to stare.

Finally, the missing bikers arrived, and a consensus was reached that allowed the woman to stay. But for what purpose? To endure more abuse? I couldn't fathom why she would want to be there, but it became clear that she would do anything to become an old lady and wear the patch. She made advances toward any brother who would have her, which didn't sit well with the other sisters. They considered her trash and treated her accordingly. My heart ached for her, caught in a web of her own making.

As Sherri, the boss's old lady, approached me, I could sense her seasoned presence and authority. She wasted no time in asking if this was my first time, and her words left me momentarily puzzled. First time on a bike? First time surrounded by badass bikers? It took a moment for me to realize what she meant. "Um, no. I've never been to a 1%ers clubhouse before. This is all new to me. It's my first rodeo," I replied, feeling a mix of curiosity and apprehension.

Sherri's response clarified that my inexperience was noticeable. She advised me to stick close to her, follow her lead, and offered some straightforward instructions: "Don't get drunk and don't ask questions. If you see anything you shouldn't be seeing, shut the hell up about it." It was an odd and somewhat jarring directive, leaving me wondering what I might encounter and why it should remain a secret.

I realized then that I had been naive about the true nature of this MC. Roxy had misled me, and the riding club Johnny was previously a part of was nothing like what I was now experiencing. The level of secrecy and control within this MC was a world apart from anything I had known or witnessed before.

PROPERTY OF THE KING

Observing the old ladies within this tight-knit group, I had an eye-opening revelation. There was an unspoken pecking order among them. Some were loyal partners to the MC brothers, bound by marriage or long-standing relationships. Others held elevated status by association with high-ranking brothers, those holding esteemed titles or positions within the motorcycle club's hierarchy. And at the pinnacle of this hierarchy stood the boss's old lady, shouldering the heaviest responsibilities. She took charge of maintaining order within the household and ensuring that the other old ladies fulfilled their roles dutifully. This realization shed light on the intricate dynamics and unwritten rules that governed the world of the old ladies, where respect, loyalty, and the preservation of the club's traditions held paramount significance.

The bikes started pulling out from the parking lot of the gas station, two by two. We were to ride in the back of the pack because Johnny was still prospecting. Johnny tapped me on my thigh and asked, "Ready?"

"I'm as ready as I'll ever be. Let's do this," I mustered with determination in my voice. The engines roared as our bikes bolted out of the gas station. Johnny accelerated, swiftly shifting through the gears—first, second... I barely felt the transition into third or fourth. It seemed as if he seamlessly leaped into fifth gear just before merging onto the freeway entrance ramp. Johnny's focus was fixated on keeping pace with the pack, oblivious to the Suburban hurtling toward us at an alarming speed. I failed to perceive it as well. To this day, I cannot fathom how we survived that moment. It was as if God dispatched His angels, raising the Suburban above us, granting us passage beneath it. There is no other explanation for its miraculous miss. I could physically sense the metallic mass whizzing past and around me—a surreal, out-of-body experience. Everything momentarily turned to darkness. Although it likely lasted mere seconds, it felt like an eternity. Overwhelmed by the adrenaline surge, I began to dry-heave on the back of Johnny's bike.

"John, did you see that? How did we miss that collision? Pull over, I need to vomit," I pleaded, clutching onto his vest tightly from behind.

"I can't pull over, Deb. We're fine, you're fine. Stay calm, we're going to be okay," he reassured, his words competing with the roaring engines. He reached out to comfort me, his hand gently rubbing my leg as it encircled him.

"Johnny, put both hands on the bars! Stay focused, please! I'm scared, John. I'm completely terrified," I cried out, my voice a blend of anguish and fear. My emotions overflowed, tears streaming down my face as I voiced my distress. Alas, my outburst went unheard by the brothers, who remained oblivious to the near catastrophe, drowned out by the thunderous symphony of our motorcycles.

The clubhouse was situated several miles deep within a dilapidated neighborhood, where the worn-out street signs and graffiti-adorned houses whispered tales of neglect. The desolate streets were strewn with abandoned cars, some lacking tires, adding to the forlorn ambiance. As we sped past, I caught glimpses of a handful of figures lingering on street corners, their presence merely fleeting in my peripheral vision. Our destination lay ahead, beckoning us towards a vacant lot, marked by a trailer stationed at one end and a modest, shack-like outbuilding at the other. The property remained veiled behind a sturdy wooden fence, guarded by imposing gateways maneuvered by the club's vigilant enforcers, leaving the mysteries concealed within the confines of the compound.

PROPERTY OF THE KING

As the bikes pulled up to the gate, a couple of bikers got off and met with other members that were standing guard outside. They did the handshake, fist bump thing. They slapped each other on the back, turned around and gave us all the go ahead to proceed into the club property. Moments later, the gate glided open, and we rode in two by two.

As we entered the heavily guarded space, a sense of unease washed over me. The surroundings seemed far from safe, and flashes of the dramatic scenes from the FX series, Sons of Anarchy, played out in my mind. Brothers approached us as soon as we parked the bike, but I stood there, feeling overwhelmed and unsure of how to react. Sherri's voice broke through my thoughts, pulling me along with her. "Come on, honey, you can help in the kitchen," she said, leading me away. In no time, she had drinks in hand for both of us. It amazed me how swiftly she had taken care of it all. "Here, drink this. It'll make you feel better," she said, but with a warning not to drink too much, as the brothers disliked their old ladies getting drunk. It was at that moment I realized Sherri's capacity for alcohol. She never seemed intoxicated by the amount that she drank.

I followed Sherri into a worn-down mobile home, where the other women gave me a cursory glance and a brief greeting. There was no club handshake, no pat on the back, and no inquiries about who I was or where I came from. They just didn't care. Despite that, I did my best to assist with the food preparation until Sherri motioned for me to step outside. "Don't worry," she assured me. "They like you, but you don't have a PO patch on your back. They don't trust you."

"But I'm married to my husband." I held up my hand to show off my wedding ring. "Doesn't that count for something? Anything?" I questioned, hoping that my commitment to Johnny would carry some weight.

"Oh, honey. See that brother over there, standing by the fire pit?" Sherri pointed to a man engrossed in physical intimacy with a woman who clearly wasn't his wife. "You'd think he was with his wife, right?" she continued.

I nodded, the scene before me leaving me disgusted and disheartened.

"That's a stripper from the club up the street. His wife was here last night," Sherri revealed.

"And the other women in this club are okay with that? Are you okay with that?" I asked, struggling to comprehend the apparent acceptance of such behavior.

"We don't talk about it," Sherri replied cryptically.

Her words hit me hard. This was what she had been trying to convey all along. Keep quiet about the actions of the brothers, even if it affected the old ladies. It was a bunch of crap, I thought to myself. I couldn't fathom keeping my mouth shut in the face of such situations. The thought of some other woman's lips on my Johnny's neck sent a surge of protectiveness through me. Lights out, indeed.

"Who's the woman standing over there?" I pointed while I asked.
"Put your finger down. You never point at an old lady or her old man. Especially when he's the boss of the 1%ers and she's his old lady."

"Oh, she's pretty," I said. For some reason, I felt a strange pull towards her. I wanted to know her. I wanted to pick her brain about all this club business. She seemed like a nice woman. After watching her for some time, I thought I would introduce myself. "I'm going to go over there and say hi," I said.

PROPERTY OF THE KING

"Oh, no you're not! Don't even think about it. She won't talk to you without a PO patch on your back. Don't go over there." I probably should have listened, but Sherri got caught up in another conversation and left me sitting next to the fire by myself. Once again, I wondered what in the hell I was doing here.

I glanced up, only to find the woman they had warned me not to engage with heading towards me. Was I expected to just sit there silently, like a fool? No, I couldn't resist introducing myself. "Hi, I'm Debbie. I'm here with Johnny. We're from Michigan, where it's freezing right now. Lots of snow. Have you ever experienced snow?" the words tumbled out of my mouth, transforming me into a babbling idiot. She looked at me, tilting her head, and responded, "Yes, I've seen snow before."

I couldn't help but feel a sense of victory—she was actually talking to me! Why wouldn't she like me? I'm kind-hearted and even somewhat funny. But then, with a smirk and a touch of arrogance, she inquired, "Your old man wears the prospect cut, right?"

"Yup, that's him. My honey," I replied.

Her smile took on a sidelong twist as she condescendingly reminded me once more of his prospect status. With a flick of her long, blonde braids, as if to say, "Screw you," she walked away.

As I reflected on my interaction with Sherri and the other women in the club, I couldn't help but feel a sense of disappointment. I had hoped for a deeper connection, perhaps even friendship, but it seemed that my presence alone wasn't enough to earn their acceptance. I questioned the significance of Sherri's position as an old lady within the club. If she wasn't merely another old lady, what made her different?

Back at our condo, I shared my experience with Johnny, expressing my frustration about not being embraced by the women, particularly the boss's wife. I couldn't understand why I wasn't accepted, believing that I had a fun and likable personality. Seeking some clarity, I turned to Johnny for answers.

"John, you know she would like me, right? I mean, come on, I'm fun. I don't get it," I voiced my concerns, hoping for some reassurance.

"Debbie, just relax," Johnny responded, attempting to ease my worries. "Hang out, listen to Sherri. She knows this world better than you do. Trust her."

Although my feelings were hurt initially, I understood Johnny's perspective. He believed Sherri held valuable insights and wisdom about the club's dynamics. I realized that building relationships and winning the friendship of these women would require more time and patience. I resolved to keep an open mind and seize future opportunities to connect with them during our stay in Florida. After all, I was determined to navigate this unfamiliar territory and understand the complex dynamics of the club, even if it meant stepping out of my comfort zone.

The next evening was "bike night." I couldn't help but feel a surge of excitement. The ride downtown was exhilarating, albeit less intense than the previous night. We navigated the neighborhood streets instead of the freeway, maintaining a high speed but with heightened awareness of our surroundings. It was a thrilling experience. The streets were alive with energy, blocked off for the occasion. The sound of lively bands filled the air, and a myriad of vendors offered unique merchandise. It was an impressive experience, promising an evening of pure enjoyment.

PROPERTY OF THE KING

Amongst the bustling atmosphere, a couple of brothers from the 1%ers invited Johnny to join them at a table located outside of a restaurant. It was an enticing opportunity to immerse himself in the vibrant scene and perhaps further establish connections within the MC. Eager to explore and embrace the rebel spirit, I eagerly joined them.

I felt a sense of rebellion walking around with this intimidating group of individuals and their partners. We drew attention, with curious gazes from onlookers who observed us from a distance.

We were together for a few drinks, but before long, the suggestion arose that it was time to make our way to the strip joint.

"Oh joy, another strip joint," I muttered sarcastically to Johnny as I climbed onto the back of the bike. Strip clubs were never my scene, but I was being dragged to them more often than I liked. I couldn't help but feel sorry for the women working there. I couldn't fathom how they could be comfortable with strangers touching and groping them. It disgusted me. Intoxicated men, likely with their wives waiting at home for them to return, while their clammy, fat hands were all over another woman's body. That was only what was visible on the surface. Who knew what went on behind closed doors, adorned with signs reading "Private Lap Dance in Session"?

It rarely took long for the managers or owners of these joints to hate on me. I usually got a glass of water, because by the time we arrived, I was exhausted and ready for bed. Staying out until two or three in the morning was considered early for my new friends, but very late for me. I just wanted to go home.

Most nights at the strip joint followed a familiar pattern. I would find myself perched at the end of the bar alongside Johnny, and inexplicably, the dancers seemed drawn to me. Not to smother me with their over-the-top, silicone-enhanced bosoms, but rather to engage in conversation. I would listen attentively, offering words of encouragement, gently suggesting that they deserved better. In my own way, I sought to impart a sense of self-respect upon them. Reflecting on those moments now, I can't help but wonder what they must have thought of me. Here I was, associating with a group of bikers who often viewed women as second-class citizens, yet I was offering guidance and advice to them. At least they were compensated for their performances. Most women possessed undeniable beauty, and once I started talking with them, I could understand how they found themselves in this situation. Together, we would brainstorm ways in which they could escape this lifestyle, freeing themselves from the burden of guilt and shame that weighed them down. Some sought solace in drugs and alcohol, using them as a temporary escape from their own self-perception. It's no wonder the club owners usually held a disdainful opinion of me. I was perceived as a threat, potentially derailing their profit-making endeavors by leading these women towards a more fulfilling way of life.

I don't know if I ever got through to any of the women I met at the strip clubs. Had I known Jesus like I do now, I would have shared the gospel with them. I'd have had a better chance of helping them. I hope they could feel the love I felt for them, which was nowhere near the love they thought they were getting from the fat, bald, sweaty old men shoving dollar bills in the string tied around their waist that they called panties.

That night in Florida, I followed Johnny into the strip club and found vacant barstools pulled under a stage the strippers were performing on. I sat down on the first stool and pulled the other out for Johnny. Just then, one of his brothers pulled him aside to have a private conversation.

Johnny assured me, "Stay here. I'll be right back." While waiting, I noticed a woman with a fuller figure wrapped around a pole on the stage in front of me. Her attire, consisting of a neon yellow string holding her bottoms in place, caught my attention. Despite her size, she displayed impressive dance moves.

Taking a moment to divert my gaze from her thighs that were wrapped around the pole, I called out, "Hey, Johnny... could you get me another drink? Make it a double, please." I wasn't in the mood for a mere bottle of water.

"So... it's cold in Michigan, huh?" Pulling out the empty stool next to me was the old lady of the boss of the 1%er whom I was told not to talk to the night before. She set a shot of whiskey and butterscotch schnapps in front of me. I wanted to tell her I didn't drink shots, and I also didn't think it was a good idea to mix whiskey with gin, but something was telling me to suck it up and quit being a Debbie downer.

I raised my shot glass to hers and yelled, "Cheers to warm weather."

"My name's Susie and that's my husband, Axe."

She shared more information about herself and her family. "I'm an accountant, a CPA. Axe owns his own construction company," she continued, sharing some details about her husband. "And we have two kids. Our son is heading off to college in the fall, aiming to become a doctor. Oh, and our daughter recently achieved the prestigious title of Prom Queen."

As I listened to her words, a thought crossed my mind. This situation feels strangely familiar, but with a twist. Normally, it's the strippers who open up about their pasts, not the wives of the bosses. Ah, the unpredictability of life, even in strip clubs.

This is one of the many reasons I got so sucked into this MC life. There are professional people who are members. They own businesses. They're doctors, lawyers, professors. I've always held the utmost respect for people in positions like this. Probably stemming from my shortcomings in school, I gave people too much credit based on their professions, rather than who they were based on their character. Being close to the club—albeit in its second-class position—I learned fast that people with degrees and businesses can be just as corrupt and shady, if not more so, than the average Joe. But back then, when I learned this information about Susie and Axe, it encouraged me to believe this club life that Johnny entered would not be as bad as I feared.

Susie's revelations left me with a flurry of questions. Curiosity got the best of me as I contemplated the various aspects of her life. I couldn't help but wonder: Do her children have any inkling about her involvement in the club? Does her commitment to family always take precedence over her involvement here? Are her parents aware of this side of her life? And last, did she experience any nerves when her husband stepped up?

These inquiries tugged at my mind, reflecting the natural curiosity that arises when faced with such intriguing circumstances. Oh, the complexities of human existence! I yearned to delve deeper into Susie's story, eager to uncover the answers to these burning questions, and just like that, she was on a roll. "My kids hate that my husband is in the club. He rarely goes to their sporting events anymore. He isn't there to help them with their homework. I do all of it. He's always busy with club stuff. He's either gone, or his physical body is present, and his mind is somewhere else. He's on the phone all the time." I could relate to that. "My son hates it when his dad wears his cut to his school events. Axe didn't step up. This is the only motorcycle club he's ever been in."

"And he's already the boss?" I asked. They seemed to be such a young couple.

I asked her if she was ever worried that he'd cheat on her or become someone that she didn't know. She replied, "No! Never. He'd leave the club life before anything like that would happen. We talked about it when he was probating to become a 1%er."

Years later, I met up with Axe at a different club event in Florida. He had a girl wrapped around him that looked like she hadn't bathed in months. Her hair was stringy and dirty, hanging in her face. She gave me a toothy, or toothless, grin. "Hey girl! What's up?" She could hardly stand up. She seemed paranoid as she talked with me, while scratching and picking her face. I asked Axe where Susie was. He gave me a blank glare. It had been a while since I saw him last, but I barely recognized him. He was a mess. He looked nothing like the Axe I had met years before. What once was the body of a strong, hardworking construction owner was now one of skin and bones. He had no smile for me when I asked for the second time where his wife was. He grabbed his dirty girl and walked away.

I knew I'd catch hell for questioning him, and I did. One of the other old ladies pulled me aside and asked me about the conversation. I told her I had no respect for anyone who was cheating on his wife.

I didn't care who he was, boss or not. It didn't matter to me. It was wrong. He was wrong. Besides, I considered Susie a friend.

Later that night, Johnny confronted me, urging me to mind my own business and let the matter rest. But that didn't sit well with me. No, I couldn't simply brush it off. I had to know the truth. The other old ladies wouldn't speak a word about what happened. So, I took to Facebook and reached out to Susie, determined to unravel the mystery surrounding Axe's actions. And that's when everything unraveled. I discovered Axe had indeed been unfaithful, engaging in affairs with various women. Club whores, mommas, and sweet butts were just a few of the labels bestowed upon these "intercepting women."

My heart shattered for Susie. I couldn't help but recall our conversation from years ago, back when a stripper was boldly displaying herself before us. Susie had once asserted with unwavering certainty, "My husband will never cheat on me. He loves me and would abandon this lifestyle before that happened."

It was a poignant reminder of how the woman I was initially forbidden to speak to, someone who had intimidated me at one time, had now become a woman I was forbidden to engage with because her partner had willingly sacrificed their relationship and everything else for the allure of the life he embraced.

Chapter Nine
Momma of the House

"So that we may no longer be children, tossed to and fro by the waves and carried about by every wind of doctrine, by human cunning, by craftiness in deceitful schemes." ~ Ephesians 4:14 (ESV)

A FEW MONTHS PASSED since my return from Florida when a significant moment arrived—I was gifted with my very own "Property of" patches. Johnny made sure they were expertly sewn onto the back of my leather vest by an authorized club seamstress; it was an honor not entrusted to just anyone. The sensation of slipping into that vest for the first time, adorned with the "Property of" patches, was nothing short of exhilarating. I felt a surge of pride and accomplishment coursing through me. Finally, I had arrived! I was the epitome of coolness.

One of my first times wearing this vest with the patches was while attending a concert at a large venue, outside in the sunny state of Florida. My husband was in the middle of a conversation with a brother, and I didn't want to interrupt him, so I thought I would sneak off by myself to use the bathroom. I was surrounded by unfamiliar faces. I could feel the presence of someone following me, but I didn't know anyone there. I shrugged it off and continued to walk to the bar where I could use their bathroom.

Sure enough, when I walked out of the bathroom, I saw one of Johnny's brothers leaning against the wall, waiting for me, "protecting" me without my even knowing it.

Another time at a different concert, I had two MC members on "Debbie watching duty." I thought it would be fun to try to escape their protection. Two big guys. One on each side of me. Watching and waiting. I ducked down and got out of their sight. From the view I had, I could see them, but they couldn't see me. They kept scanning the room for yours truly. Sweat was falling from the bigger guy's brow and each one was blaming the other for losing me. They knew they would be in trouble if they came back without me. I tapped them on the shoulder from behind with a big smile on my face. "What's up guys? Lose something?" I said. They weren't too happy with me, but never said a word about it to Johnny. They knew if they couldn't keep an eye on me, they probably wouldn't be trusted to watch the clubhouse or their brothers. Nobody wanted to be on "Debbie duty."

Knowing what I know now, I should have never messed around with these guys that were trying to protect me. Being an independent, strong-willed woman, it drove me nuts that I had to have someone always following me around. It was a hard fact that I needed protection and that I would have to get used to it if I wanted to wear the patches and travel with my husband. Rival clubs could mess with me to get to my husband. I was considered the club's property, so in other clubs' eyes, I was fair game. And because of this, I always needed protection.

I earned a special nickname from John's chapter's old ladies—they affectionately referred to me as "Momma of the house." It was a title that carried weight and respect, even acknowledged by some of the hang-arounds who began calling me Momma as well. The term "Momma" held a special place in my heart. I embraced it wholeheartedly, as it symbolized my dedication to taking care of the chapter's needs. Men and women alike could rely on me for various tasks within the clubhouse. From organizing food for parties to tending to mundane chores like emptying ashtrays and cleaning, I made it my mission to ensure everyone felt comfortable and well cared for. I wanted to set myself apart from other old ladies in the club, determined to wield the influence that came with being the boss's old lady. Whether the men in the MC acknowledged it openly or not, there was a certain power that accompanied my position. And slowly, that power fed my ego.

As the Momma of the house, I discovered the art of manipulation, using it to shape situations and influence people to bring about desired outcomes. I became privy to conversations and information that Johnny needed to know, earning the trust of others who shared things they wouldn't dare disclose to my old man or fellow old ladies. I witnessed things that should have remained hidden, and I took it upon myself to approach Johnny with problems that others feared to confront him about. It was an intoxicating role, and I reveled in it during the first year of receiving my patches.

One of my responsibilities as Momma of the house was to maintain order among the women, and sometimes that meant dealing with difficult situations. One instance stands out in my memory, involving Amy, the wife of one of the brothers. She struggled with addiction to prescription pills and street drugs, particularly Vicodin. Mix that with whiskey, and it was a recipe for disaster.

During a visit to another clubhouse, my old man pulled me aside and asked me to keep an eye on Amy while he and her husband attended a meeting. She was completely intoxicated. Amy wasn't my responsibility; she wasn't my monkey, and this certainly wasn't my circus. Yet, she continued to cause a scene, verbally berating a couple of brothers, criticizing their clubhouse and drinks. Her behavior did not shock me. She could barely stand, and I knew if I didn't intervene, both her old man and mine would have to face the consequences of her actions. I questioned why this fell on my shoulders, but perhaps it was just part of the Momma's job. Maybe it was, in fact, my circus.

Amy shouted at a brother in the chapter's house, refusing to clean up her mess and telling him to do it himself. I rushed over, yelling "No, no, no!" I apologized to the brother, explaining that Amy was heavily intoxicated, which was clear from her erratic behavior. She was bouncing off the walls, her dilated pupils giving her an almost demonic appearance. Finally, she crashed into a chair.

"Chill out," I said. "What's wrong with you? You know you can't talk like that. You're going to get your old man in trouble."

"Good, he deserves it. I hate him," she slurred.

Later that night, back at the hotel, Amy and her husband got into a heated argument. Johnny and I attempted to mediate, but she was too far gone to comprehend our words. It was futile to reason with her in that state. She was in her underwear, screaming at the top of her lungs, snot running down her nose, mascara smearing her face. She even threw punches at her old man. Johnny tried to restrain her from this, while we tried to talk her off the cliff.

Her husband was devastated, and for the first time, I saw him break down in tears. This tough biker was brought to his knees by the woman he loved. We were at a loss for what to do. Eventually, Amy passed out on the floor and slept there for the night. Her husband,

PROPERTY OF THE KING

Johnny, and I agreed I would take her to a treatment center the next morning.

The following morning, while her husband and Johnny went off to a club meeting, it became my responsibility once again to handle this mess. I made my way to her room, finding her already attempting to calm her trembling hands by downing a beer. She had taken a couple of pills as I approached her.

"I'm not going anywhere," she declared. "I have kids at home. Who's going to take care of them?" Her eyes darkened, consumed by inner demons. I knew that look all too well. She was angry and started to cry. "You think my old man is this wonderful guy. You think I'm a piece of crap. He's just as messed up as I am!" she screamed, her pain and frustration pouring out.

My heart ached for her, witnessing the brokenness that consumed her. I longed to be the catalyst for her healing, to mend the shattered pieces of her life. With genuine concern, I reached out with support and encouragement. "Don't worry," I reassured her, my voice filled with optimism. "You're not alone in this. Johnny and I will take care of your kids. It's crucial that you seek help. You deserve a life that isn't this hard. Your children need you, and I want to help you get there." I tried my best to infuse positivity into every word, hoping that my sincerity would resonate and inspire her to accept my offer.

"Screw that. I don't have the problem. My old man does. If he's not getting help, then I'm not getting help. Take me home."

And so, I found myself in the position of driving her back home, enduring the agonizing two-hour journey filled with her outbursts of yelling, screaming, and inconsolable tears. It was an experience I wouldn't soon forget. I must confess, though, that I made a tough decision that day. As much as I hate to admit it, I left her at home with her children, who had grown accustomed to witnessing such manic episodes. Overwhelmed by the weight of it all, I dialed Johnny's number, seeking guidance on what to do next.

"Leave her there," he responded.

Doing what I was told to do, I drove away, attempting to convince myself that her children had unfortunately become accustomed to this turmoil throughout their lives. I rationalized that it wasn't my fault, and that there was little I could do to alter the circumstances. This was not my burden to bear, not my circus to tame. Nevertheless, a lingering sense of sorrow enveloped me, as I couldn't help but empathize deeply with everyone involved in this heart-wrenching situation.

The role of being Momma of the house turned out to be far from glamorous. There was no glory in it, only a growing sense of darkness that gradually engulfed me. The naivety I once held had dissipated, replaced by a somber understanding of the reality I found myself in.

Deep down, I knew this wasn't what I desired anymore, but I felt trapped, unsure of how to break free from these shackles. Something within me felt off, tainted even. A profound sense of shame replaced the once-prideful feeling when I attempted to persuade women to don the "Property of" patch. As Momma of the house, it was my responsibility to convince other old ladies to wear the vest proudly. However, some women resisted, expressing their feelings of degradation and control to their old men. Their old men sent them to me, expecting me to deliver the same hollow speech Roxy had given me when Johnny first joined the club: "You should be proud to wear this. It offers protection." I recited the words, but deep down, I knew it was all an elaborate, ugly lie. It was all just empty rhetoric.

Fortunately, because of the small size of Johnny's chapter, I didn't have to persuade many women to wear the "Property of" patch. But the interactions I had with them served as reminders of the complexities beneath the surface. Each woman had her own story, shaped by her experiences and circumstances. It made me reflect on the importance of empathy and understanding, and how the club could serve as both a refuge and a trap for those seeking solace and belonging.

It struck me as ironic how I'd worry about the plight of strippers and the degrading nature of their work, yet I tried to convince other women to become someone's "Property." The shift in my perspective was drastic. The pride I once felt while wearing the "Property of" vest had now transformed into a profound sense of absurdity and stupidity. I felt controlled, debased, and foolish for even buying into such a demeaning concept.

There was an unsettling stirring inside me, a voice that whispered that something was fundamentally wrong with it all. I grew weary of the façade of being Momma of the house. It was a stark contrast from my earlier aspirations of never wanting women to experience what I went through back in Florida when I longed to be part of the old lady club. I tried to be outgoing and friendly towards most of the women I encountered, even though there were some who seemed impenetrable, their tough exteriors shielding the pain they carried from untold hardships. For some of these women, the club became their chosen family, their sole support system. They clung tightly to their old man; this was their world.

Yet, I yearned for them to feel intimidated by me and the "Property of" vest I wore. I had become the very thing I despised. It's challenging to recognize this when you're deeply immersed in the midst of it all, when you're entangled in the complexities of the lifestyle. But deep down, I knew I had to reconnect with God. I needed to find my identity in Christ, not as an old lady in an MC.

Unbeknownst to me at the time, the unsettling feeling stirring within me was the voice of God calling me to something greater. He had plans for my life that extended far beyond being labeled as someone's property within a club. God desired me to be His property, to belong to Him alone. He was revealing to me the wrongness of this lifestyle, its foundation built upon sin. During Johnny's absences, fulfilling his duties for the club, I made a conscious decision to stay home instead of constantly attending parties and events at clubhouses with him. The fear of missing out on the excitement gradually dissipated. Our lives shifted from "club-life is everything" to acknowledging that his club was his own, while I embarked on the journey of living my own life, guided by a higher purpose.

Chapter Ten

God's Unrelenting Pursuit

"For the son of man came to seek and to save the lost." ~ Luke 19:10 (ESV)

It was Easter Sunday, a day filled with significance and meaning. Yet, Johnny was once again away on "club business," leaving me alone. I'd grown accustomed to his frequent absences on weekends, but this particular day felt different. My parents were out of town visiting my brother's family, and my son showed no interest in acknowledging the holiday. I found myself isolated, devoid of the joyous celebrations and family traditions that typically filled Easter.

The ache in my heart intensified as I scrolled through social media, witnessing my friends happily preparing meals with their loved ones, mothers taking their children to local Easter egg hunts, and the sight of adorable little girls in their beautiful Easter dresses. It had been quite some time since Johnny and I attended church together, despite both of us being raised in the Roman Catholic faith and sharing the same beliefs. Easter held immense significance for us both, as it symbolized the resurrection of Jesus Christ—His ultimate sacrifice for our sins, His burial, and His triumphant resurrection on the third day. Christ's redemptive work destroyed the power of sin and paved the way for a personal relationship with God. Johnny and I both loved to celebrate Easter.

In that moment, I realized the depth of the void in my life, the longing for a connection to something greater than the MC and its distractions. The significance of Easter reminded me of the profound sacrifice Jesus made on my behalf and the opportunity it offered for a renewed relationship with God. My heart stirred with a longing for a different fulfillment, one that couldn't be found within the confines of the club lifestyle.

In the past, I had experienced a similar sense of marginalization within the church as I did with Johnny's motorcycle club. I felt like a second-rate citizen, excluded from fully participating in the sacraments. The reason behind this exclusion was that I hadn't gone through the "annulment process" for my first marriage. I struggled to comprehend how a mere piece of paper could nullify the significance of my previous commitment. It seemed arbitrary and disconnected from the essence of my faith.

Though I didn't fully understand the theological reasons behind the annulment process, I was made acutely aware of the judgment and treatment I received from others within the church. For example, I would sit quietly in the pew, head bowed, while those deemed righteous would pass by, receiving the sacraments of Communion. Leaving the church, I often carried a heavy burden of shame and guilt. Being divorced and not seeking an annulment placed me in a category of sinners, viewed differently by the church community. Their inability to comprehend my perspective and my choice not to pursue an annulment only intensified this divide.

I faithfully received most of my sacraments within the church as a child, believing that by doing so, I fulfilled all the requirements for God's love and acceptance. However, the treatment I received and the sense of exclusion I felt challenged my perception. I questioned whether my worthiness and relationship with God were truly contingent upon fulfilling these external obligations. The disconnect between the teachings of the Bible and the way I was treated fueled my inner turmoil. Deep down, I longed for a genuine understanding of God's love and acceptance that transcended the judgments and barriers imposed by others.

GOD NEVER LEFT ME

Soon after marrying Johnny, I began sensing a tug to reconnect with the church. It felt like God was gently nudging me. We believed it was important to raise our son in church, and since both Johnny and I were familiar with the Catholic faith, we decided to stay connected to it.

However, being back in the church didn't bring the sense of fulfillment I'd hoped for. My relationship with God was strained during that time. I went through the motions, simply checking off a box on a list in case something happened to me. I longed to experience true grace and wanted to ensure my son's spiritual upbringing.

Despite my reservations, the feeling persisted, leading me to enroll in adult classes to receive the final sacrament of confirmation that I didn't receive as a young adult. This sacrament, viewed by the Catholic Church as a way to strengthen one's baptismal vows as an adult and openly accept Jesus into their life, seemed like a meaningful step. Graduation day was meant to be a joyous occasion, but a phone call from the class teacher shattered my excitement. She became fixated on the "church laws" and discovered that I hadn't gotten an annulment for my previous marriage. I couldn't help but question why I could marry without confirmation in the first place. This revelation only fueled the teacher's anger, and I was informed that I couldn't proceed with confirmation until I obtained an annulment. The weight of sin, shame, and guilt intensified.

I felt a mix of anger, hurt, and disappointment. It seemed ridiculous, as the focus was on church laws rather than the will of God. In that moment, my heart hardened, and I defiantly shouted my frustrations into the phone with this woman that was supposed to help me receive the sacrament of my confirmation. Determined to express my viewpoint, I scheduled an appointment with the priest to present my case. I couldn't understand why I needed a piece of paper to confirm my forgiveness. Nowhere in the Bible does it specify such a requirement. I recognized my own flaws and the need for repentance, trusting in God's forgiveness. None of it made sense to me, and the priest's lack of agreement left me disheartened. He dismissed my opinion, emphasizing that it was a matter of church law that I should respect.

Disgusted by the situation, I confided in John, expressing my desire to quit the church. However, he gently reminded me we were CCD teachers (Confraternity of Christian Doctrine, which is a religious education program in the Catholic Church), and that we still wanted our son to receive his sacraments. I felt trapped, caught between my own convictions and the responsibility we had undertaken.

PROPERTY OF THE KING

ENOUGH IS ENOUGH

It was Ash Wednesday, the first day of Lent, a significant observance for Catholics and some Protestant denominations. On the weekend preceding Ash Wednesday, a heart-wrenching event unfolded in our lives. Johnny and I experienced a miscarriage, a profound loss that shook us to the core. We had embarked on a challenging journey of in vitro fertilization, investing time, money, and emotions into our hope for a child. The process involved tests, shots, moments of disappointment, countless appointments, and finally, a glimmer of hope. I was pregnant! We were thrilled. Unfortunately, the hope and dreams we had of being parents again were shattered by the devastating news of losing our precious baby boy. It was a painful blow, compounded by the realization that we had exhausted our financial resources and emotional strength to continue with in vitro fertilization ever again.

As Ash Wednesday approached, we found solace in the thought of attending Mass and seeking support from our church community. The service was intensely emotional for both of us. Afterward, Johnny, sensing my profound sadness, gently suggested staying to talk with the priest, hoping he could offer prayers and insight into the inexplicable tragedy we had just endured. Numb with grief, I simply nodded, unable to find my voice.

Walking hand in hand, we approached the altar, tears streaming down my face. Johnny took the lead in addressing the priest, his voice trembling with vulnerability. He shared, "Father, we recently lost our baby, and we're struggling. Could you please pray with us and help us understand?" In an instant, the priest's expression shifted from curiosity to frustration, and his response dripped with irritation. "No, you'll have to call the office tomorrow and arrange a meeting with my secretary. It's been a long day, and I'm tired." I continued to sob, my shoulders trembling uncontrollably. Johnny, at a loss for words, held me tightly, his eyes filled with disbelief. He managed to reply, "Okay," but it seemed the priest had already turned his back on us, oblivious to Johnny's response as he walked away.

Thankfully, the church's deacon witnessed the exchange and immediately approached us. Sensing our distress, he embraced us and apologized for the priest's behavior. He kindly invited us to his home, just a short drive away, where he and his wife could pray with us in a more intimate setting.

That night, surrounded by the compassion of the deacon and his wife, I began to comprehend that I could lean on the Lord during my darkest moments. While I may never fully understand the reasons behind such tragedies in this world, I found solace in knowing that God holds the answers. The deacon's love and care were evident, yet Johnny and I both recognized that this experience marked the end of our connection with "The Church," as we knew it.

SEARCHING

We gradually drifted away from attending Mass and turned towards worldly pursuits for fulfillment. Our lives revolved around material possessions, driving fancy cars and living in beautiful homes. The church became increasingly distant, with only occasional visits on important holidays, such as Easter and Christmas.

PROPERTY OF THE KING

During this time, I found peace and a connection with God while running ultra-marathons in the woods. The serene trails beneath the canopy of trees became a sanctuary where I poured out my heart to Him. Despite maintaining a relationship with God, I had allowed other idols to take precedence in my life.

Curiosity led me to explore Buddhism through friendships with practicing Buddhists. Their inner peace and non-judgmental attitudes intrigued me. I took part in chanting, drumming, and even attending events at temples or home altars. As I delved deeper into this practice, I realized it was leading me further away from the truth. I was trying to blend Buddhism with Christianity, idolizing Buddha while claiming to be a Christian. I knew deep down that it was wrong, and I needed to return to God.

Once again, I sought peace in the woods, running for miles on dirt trails, searching for answers about my identity and God's true nature. I was lost, unsure of what to believe anymore. The pain inflicted by the church had created confusion and division within me, eroding my inner peace. Unbeknownst to me at the time, the Holy Spirit was actively working in my life, guiding me towards God's truth amid the world's lies and confusion.

As for my marriage, it was functional but not thriving. I would rate it a seven out of ten. I wasn't fulfilling the role of a submissive wife and my husband didn't love me as Christ loves the church. We lacked a true understanding of what love really is. From the outside, our marriage seemed idyllic, and some even envied what they perceived we had. Little did they know I had threatened Johnny with divorce multiple times throughout the year.

DEBORAH MCKINZIE

A NEW HEART

Feeling alone, I went to see "The Case for Christ" playing at the local movie theater. During the movie, I became emotional, and I noticed another woman crying in front of me. We both expressed how great the movie was and decided to grab a drink and talk. She suggested coffee at McDonald's, but I mentioned getting a glass of wine instead. She explained that she didn't drink and again suggested coffee at McDonald's.

On the drive to McDonald's, I called Johnny to tell him about the movie and my unexpected plan to meet someone I barely knew to talk about God. He found it strange but didn't object. Although I didn't have a relationship with God, I always loved talking about Him, and this woman seemed kind. Our conversation over coffee flowed effortlessly, as if we had been friends forever. She told me about her church in town, which I initially viewed with skepticism. When she asked if I attended church, I defensively responded that I didn't believe church attendance was necessary for a relationship with God. She gently mentioned that the Bible encourages believers to be in communion with one another. I tried to lighten the mood with a joke about trees being my communion, but she didn't grasp it.

Although I had heard about her church and pastor before, guilt and shame had prevented me from visiting. She extended an invitation for me to attend with her, and I thought it wouldn't hurt to try it. If it didn't resonate with me, I could simply refrain from going again. I had nothing to lose.

PROPERTY OF THE KING

On Sunday morning, I woke up panicked, unsure about what to wear and whether I should go. I couldn't remember her name, adding to my apprehension. After multiple outfit changes, I settled on a floral dress and cream-colored heels, a departure from my usual biker attire for sure. Before leaving, I looked at myself in the mirror, prayed to God, while expressing my nervousness to Him as if He were standing right next to me.

As I entered the church, I noticed people wearing jeans and baseball caps, seemingly unaware that it was Easter Sunday. I couldn't help but judge their attire, contrasting it with the formal dress code I had grown up with. The greeter welcomed me with a cheerful "Happy Easter." I continued walking through the front doors of the church but felt apprehensive.

Inside the sanctuary, people were drinking coffee or water, something I found surprising, and wondered if the priest was aware of it. In the church of my upbringing, even chewing bubble gum was prohibited. The music began, resembling a concert. A woman played the grand piano, accompanied by guitar players, a drummer, and singers. It was a far cry from the solemn music I was accustomed to.

People around me started raising their hands and singing along with the lyrics displayed on large screens at the front. It all seemed unfamiliar and strange. Suddenly, I began sobbing uncontrollably, something rare for me. I tried to calm myself, telling myself to stop crying, but the tears only flowed harder. I felt embarrassed and tried to find some tissues or an exit in the hallway.

To my surprise, I bumped into a couple of clients from the salon who noticed my distress and asked if I was okay. I couldn't explain what was happening, and they kindly invited me to sit with them. Each of them sat on either side of me, offering comfort.

When the music stopped, a tall, lean man walked onto the stage, wearing jeans and a plaid shirt. I asked my friends if he was the priest, but they clarified that he was the pastor and that their church didn't have priests. My tone turned harsh as I inquired about his attire on Easter Sunday, expecting something more formal. They explained it wasn't about what he wore, but about his gift of preaching.

The sermon the pastor delivered that day was unforgettable. It touched me deeply and changed my life forever. After the service, my friends accompanied me to meet the pastor, who introduced himself as Alex. Overwhelmed with emotions, I cried again and felt a sense of panic. I'd never been to a church other than the Catholic one I grew up in, and I wasn't sure if attending a different denomination was sinful. The pastor shared more of the gospel with me and even gifted me with a study Bible.

Grateful for his words and his gift, tears continued to flow as I thanked him. It was then that I realized my guilt didn't come from attending a different church, but from not knowing the truth until that very day. I never saw the woman from McDonald's again, but I am forever grateful for her simple invitation to join her for church.

On that day, I was saved and filled with the Holy Spirit. It wasn't because of anything I'd done or my ability to obey rules or receive sacraments. I was saved because of God's boundless mercy and grace for me. The guilt I had felt melted away, replaced by a profound understanding of God's love and forgiveness.

The experience reminded me of Isaiah 1:18 (ESV), where God invites us to come and be cleansed, transforming our scarlet sins into pure white.

From that day forward, my life took a new direction as I embraced my newfound faith and embarked on a journey of growing closer to God. I needed to call my Johnny.

I whispered into the phone, my voice trembling with emotion, "It was so good, Honey." The tears streamed down my face uncontrollably. Johnny's concern was noticeable in his voice as he asked, "What's wrong, Hun?" But it wasn't a matter of what was wrong. It was about what was so undeniably right.

Chapter Eleven

Embracing the Light in the Darkness

"But the Lord is faithful, and He will strengthen you and protect you from the evil one." ~2 Thessalonians 3:3 (NIV)

GOD BEGAN TO PURSUE me relentlessly. His presence consumed my thoughts more often than not. I couldn't escape Him. It became increasingly difficult for me to engage in events at the clubhouse and witness the activities taking place. Worse yet, I found it challenging to be a part of it all.

I vividly recall one Saturday morning when my thoughts centered on the "Property Of" vest I wore. Having just returned from a long run, I decided—no more. I refused to go along with it any longer. I wasn't the property of the club or my husband. Gathering all the clothing associated with the club: t-shirts, hoodies, hats—I tossed them into the fire pit a few feet from our home. I doused the pile of black fabric with gasoline, struck a match, and watched with a sense of satisfaction as the flames consumed them. After a moment, I turned back towards the house, completely calm. I told my husband, "I'm heading to the grocery store. Keep an eye on the fire outside."

"What fire?" he asked.

"The one I just lit outside," I replied. He rushed to the window to witness the blaze. I explained that I was done with club life. I didn't feel angry or upset, as I might have in the past. I had reached a breaking point. He inquired about what I did with my vest, and I knew better than to destroy it. If I damaged or destroyed the "Property of" patches, Johnny would face consequences, and I didn't want that for him. So, I returned the vest to him, respectfully. Little did I know that he never turned it in. He left it untouched in the back of his closet.

It would be nice to conclude the story here—just like that. The end. Perhaps leaving you with the impression that, by God's grace, I remained free from the darkness and never returned to club life. But that would be far from the truth. Call it fear of missing out (FOMO, as the kids say), or perhaps a lingering desire to be part of the darkness. I didn't stay away for long. Johnny had to attend yet another funeral, but this one was different. It was a massive event honoring a founding member of the club. A legend, as the brothers would say. If you didn't know better, you might even call him an OG, an original gangster.

As Johnny and I were leaving our house for Florida, he tossed my "Property of" vest at me—my cut.

"What's this?" I asked, assuming he had returned it to the club when I burned the rest of my club-related belongings. I didn't want to wear it; I felt conflicted. I wanted to be part of the club, but I no longer wanted to be labeled as someone's property.

"Why do I have to wear it?" I met other wives who had distanced themselves from their husbands' club life and occasionally showed up at parties without their vests. Why couldn't I do the same?

"You know why, Deb. It's for your protection when we're out of town," he explained. I didn't like it, but I knew this to be true. If I wanted to accompany Johnny, I needed to wear the vest for my safety. Once again, I felt trapped. What's worse, I questioned why my husband would put me in a position where I needed this kind of protection.

The funeral was an enormous gathering of brothers, larger than anything I had witnessed before. The Florida State Police escorted us to the cemetery, and the number of motorcycles present was staggering. After struggling to find a place to park our bike, we made our way towards the gravesite. It felt surreal. We were not part of the immediate family, who occupied white chairs surrounding the casket. If it were a concert, we would have been in the nosebleed section—that's how far back we were. The priest arrived to commemorate this man's life, and I imagine he shared kind words, but I couldn't hear a thing. We were lost in the sea of leather, positioned too far away.

Hovering above us was a helicopter with a man strapped in, defying gravity like a circus performer, capturing photos of us with a lens capable of zooming in on the moon. Curious, I whispered to Johnny, "What's all this about?"

"FBI," he replied.

"Great," I muttered. I began contemplating the life this man had lived, the grief displayed by his brothers, and the helicopters hovering above. He had obviously engaged in shady dealings to attract such attention. I wondered if he knew where he was headed. Heaven or Hell? Did such concerns trouble him during his lifetime? Did he receive his sacraments where he found salvation in Jesus? I prayed that he had. I wouldn't wish the damnation of hell even on my worst enemies.

This experience made me ponder my relationship with the Lord and my involvement with the club. It was becoming increasingly challenging to maintain both. Could I continue to strike a balance? Was God calling me to be a beacon of light amidst the darkness? Perhaps that's what this gangster had done. If he could have a funeral with a priest and remain a part of the 1%ers, why couldn't I live this double life?

I started bringing up God more often in conversations with my friends in the club. Whenever I was around, women began seeking intimate discussions with me—women who had been hurt by the church, just like me. Those who were enduring abuse and yearned to escape their husbands. Ladies who felt they couldn't bear any more pain. Women who had grown up without fathers in their lives. I heard their stories, and I spoke to each one of them about God.

I even engaged in extensive conversations about God with a respected member of the club, someone high in the chain of command. He would say, "Yeah, that f'ing Jesus was a cool cat. He had all those f'ing Apostles, and they went around healing people and shit." Although I didn't encounter him often, whenever our paths crossed, I met him where he was in his relationship with the Lord. We discussed God, his struggles with addiction, and how he managed to stay sober in the life he led. God was opening doors and presenting me with opportunities to talk about Him. At the time, I didn't realize that this was what you call discipleship.

Chapter Twelve

Deception

"Lying lips are an abomination to the Lord, but those who act faithfully are his delight." ~ Proverbs 12:22 (ESV)

THE TRANSFORMING POWER OF the Holy Spirit enables believers to live more like Jesus and empowers them to boldly witness for Him. I admit this transformation didn't happen overnight for me. Far from it.

When I first accepted Jesus as my Savior, I had no idea how much my life would change. Everything felt new and unfamiliar. The shame and guilt that burdened me faded away, and I fell in love with the church I was attending. I couldn't contain my excitement and would often share my experiences with anyone who would listen.

Both Johnny and my mom agreed to accompany me to one of the church services. This was a significant step for my mom, who was a devout Catholic. The service we attended was quite different from her traditional Sunday Mass.

Although Johnny wasn't at the same point in his faith journey as I was, he eagerly looked forward to the service. It had been a while since we attended church together, so having him by my side meant a lot to me.

During that week, the sermon focused on being submissive to one's husband. I groaned out loud, thinking it was time to search for a new church. The word "submissive" had negative connotations in my mind. I had grown tired of being submissive to my husband and the expectations of his MC. Now, this preacher was seemingly endorsing it while citing the Bible. I felt frustrated and misunderstood. The pastor had no idea about the life I'd been living. I wanted to run out of that service as fast as I could.

To my surprise, a smile spread across Johnny's face when he heard about the sermon topic. He settled in, fully engaged, and jokingly whispered, "Pay attention, Deb." I looked at him, shrugged, and decided to give the sermon a chance.

However, the sermon didn't unfold as either Johnny or I expected it to. In short, according to the Bible, if a husband loves his wife as Christ loves the church, then wives should submit to their husbands as long as it is not bringing them into sin. The idea was that if Johnny loved me in that sacrificial way, I should submit to him just as I would to Jesus. But the reality was far from it.

Johnny started behaving more and more like a "boss" in our marriage, adopting the same authoritative attitude he had with his club brothers. When I disagreed with him, he knew how to manipulate me to get his way. He would dismiss my concerns, saying, "Deb, it's not a big deal," or claim I was being unreasonable by saying, "You're crazy. I never said I would be home last night," or accuse me of overreacting with remarks like, "You're being nasty for no reason."

One of my cherished activities with Johnny was attending church. I always loved it, but now it held an even deeper significance as we shared this time in the community of believers. On the rare occasion when he was home on a Sunday, we would always attend church. I began forming meaningful connections both within and outside of the church. God started answering my prayers and placing people in my life who would help strengthen my relationship with Christ.

I also started attending a "gospel community" (GC) once a week. GC was a small group of church members who gathered to discuss the previous Sunday's sermon, share a meal, and foster deeper connections with one another. There were several GCs within our church, and somehow, I ended up joining the Pastor's GC. It was an intimidating experience, to say the least. But my new friends were patient with me, understanding that I'd never read the Bible before and had a lot of questions. While I didn't always receive the answers I desired, their support was unwavering. There were moments when I felt frustrated and contemplated leaving the GC. I vividly recall calling the pastor one evening to inform him of my decision. He was saddened by the news and kindly asked me to explain why.

"Sure," I replied, beginning in a calm voice that gradually escalated into loud sobs. "Last week, when I asked for prayers for a friend and started praying, Jim made fun of me."

"Debbie," the pastor interjected gently, "Jim would never make fun of you or the way you pray. I believe you may have misinterpreted his intentions."

Our conversation continued, with the pastor's patient demeanor allowing me to express my defensiveness. At first, I couldn't see it, but over time, I realized that these men in my GC group were different from the men I'd been surrounded by in the past few years. This gentleman wasn't being mean; he was just joking with me. Because of my prior experiences with men in the MC, it took me a while to find certain things humorous. Today, I consider this gentleman a dear friend and a brother in Christ.

PROPERTY OF THE KING

I loved my church, the pastor, the GC I was attending and yet, I felt as if something was attempting to undermine my faith. The closer I grew to God, the more frustrated I became.

I learned my lesson when I tried to be honest and open during a Tony Robbins "Date with Destiny" program, a seven-day event that promises to rewire your mind and transform your life. However, my efforts to connect with others seemed to backfire. After a couple of days at the event, we were divided into smaller groups to brainstorm and work through our individual reasons for being there. For me, it was about overcoming the deep-rooted belief of never being enough. As for Johnny, I wasn't sure because the program recommended that couples participate in separate groups.

Initially, things were going well. Our group exchanged social media accounts and phone numbers with each other. I particularly connected with a woman who was a police officer from Canada. We'd been working together for a couple of days when I finally shared with her about my husband's involvement in the MC. Her reaction was intense and immediate. Her eyes widened, brows furrowed, and her voice escalated as she demanded to know why I hadn't mentioned it earlier in our conversation. The forcefulness of her words sent spit flying onto my face as she yelled at me to remove her contact information from my phone. She wanted nothing to do with me, and she made that abundantly clear.

At that moment, I retorted, "Chill out, lady!" I believe if she had the authority, she would have handcuffed me for something, even though I didn't know what grounds she would have found. She promptly blocked me on all social media platforms. I tried to explain to her I wasn't part of the club—it was my husband's involvement, not mine.

But it didn't matter. She made up her mind and wanted no association with me. She continued to belittle me in front of the others for my husband's affiliation with the dangerous MC. I felt my lower lip tremble. I'd faced judgment before, but never with such severity, and never within a group of people that were together trying to improve their lives. This was the reaction I feared I might receive from any of my new friends at church. Thus, I remained silent about Johnny's involvement with the MC after this incident.

Because I was filled with the Holy Spirit, I was more convicted of my sin than ever. I naturally distanced myself from the MC. Nothing about it felt right anymore. I spent more time away from it than I did with it. There were many reasons for me to stay away at this point. The heavy presence of cigarette smoke bothered me. Seeing the strippers made me deeply sad. The girlfriends who were around when the wives were absent bothered me more than ever. The inflated egos of the men reached a point of ridiculousness, and I despised it all.

This period also marked the time when Johnny and I started heading in different directions. He immersed himself in his MC life while I delved deeper into my relationship with God. The more I attended church, the closer I became to my church community and God. Balancing both worlds wasn't easy. When someone asked about the club Johnny was in, I would offer a somewhat honest answer, but leave out a lot of details in the conversation.

With our lives going in separate directions, it became easy to overlook the things I should have paid attention to. Things that never bothered me before began to grate on my nerves. Johnny grew tired of my newfound "goody two shoes" or "holy roller" attitude, and I grew weary of his tough guy performance.

PROPERTY OF THE KING

It is often said that we draw closer to God through our struggles, as He embraces us like a loving Father. James 1:12 (ESV) reminds us, "Blessed is the man who remains steadfast under trial, for when he has stood the test, he will receive the crown of life, which God has promised to those who love him."

Little did I know the magnitude of the upcoming season that would test both our lives and our marriage. It was July 13, 2019, and my world was about to be shaken.

That Saturday morning was picturesque. It was perfect for a wedding. I woke up and reached out to touch the side of the bed where Johnny slept; it didn't surprise me to find it empty. I knew he hadn't returned from the clubhouse. I woke from a nightmare in the early hour and looked for comfort in his warm presence. Disappointment washed over me as I realized he was still absent from our bed.

I felt frustrated that Johnny wouldn't accompany me to my cousin's wedding. "I can't," he responded. "You know this, Debbie. It's our club party, and I've told you over and over that I can't be there. Don't give me a hard time about it. Just come up after the reception and pass along my greetings to your family."

He couldn't understand why I was making such a big deal out of his no-show. I'd known for months that he couldn't come, yet it still bothered me. I wanted him with me.

I reluctantly accepted his decision and continued applying a second coat of mascara to my tired eyes. While I'd been aware of the club party for months, I'd secretly hoped that Johnny would have changed his mind and at least join me for the wedding ceremony. It stung even more when the day arrived, and like countless other personal events, I attended alone. It was always a struggle to explain why Johnny wasn't by my side, resorting to saying, "But hey, he says 'Hi.'" I detested it.

Wedding ceremonies always stirred up emotions within me. Listening to the vows exchanged by the bride and groom reminded me of the beautiful promises Johnny and I once made to each other. How had our lives veered so far off course from that special day? It seemed that I was no longer the recipient of our marriage vows. The MC had taken precedence. One of the old ladies within the club once confided in me, saying, "After forgiving my husband for his countless affairs, I now feel like the MC has become his mistress, leaving me alone all the time." Johnny never had an affair, but I knew what she meant when she shared this with me.

Despite my disappointment, I made the most of the wedding reception, enjoying the company of my family. I knew I had to leave soon. I didn't want to indulge in too much alcohol, because I had to drive approximately thirty minutes to reach the clubhouse. The presence of police officers was always notable in the clubhouse's vicinity, especially during the chapter's annual party. I didn't want to end up in the back of a police car, hands cuffed, en route to jail. It would be typical of me to receive a DUI ticket when I was usually the sober one, at least during that phase of my life.

This reminded me of a situation a few months prior, when a group of us headed to a party at a clubhouse a few hours away. Johnny was speeding through one small town after another until the state police finally pulled him over. One car, then two, three, and waiting for the fourth with the canine unit. "Great," I muttered. "Now what?"

Such encounters were not unfamiliar to the MC members. They had discussed what to do when pulled over by the police in several meetings. The protocol was simple: remain silent and let the club president handle the conversation. In this case, Johnny held the title of chapter president, aka "The Boss".

Hence, it came as no surprise when Johnny instructed, "Keep your mouth shut. All of you." We found ourselves surrounded by police officers and their cars. The officer inquired if John was the boss (they had a way of knowing by observing who led the pack), to which Johnny answered, "Yes, officer. I am."

"Keep your hands on the handlebars," the officer commanded. "All of you. Do not remove your hands from the bars." Meanwhile, I and the other women were asked to keep our hands on top of our bikers' shoulders. Initially, it didn't seem like a big deal, but after a couple of hours sitting in that position in scorching 90-degree weather, wearing my leather ensemble, it took a toll on my body. I was the only one wearing a helmet and asked the officer after a few minutes if I could take it off. "Not yet. Keep your hands on his shoulders," he replied.

An officer began asking the usual questions: "Are you carrying any weapons? Do you have any drugs with you?" It was no secret that some club members had guns and perhaps a few joints here and there. At that time, possessing or smoking pot was illegal in Michigan. I was unaware of any other drug they may have had on them. We waited anxiously for what felt like an eternity for the fourth police car to arrive with the drug-sniffing dog. Meanwhile, another officer went around to the bikes, photographing each biker and their old ladies with their front and back patches. I smiled as he took my picture, wondering where it would end up.

Finally, the canine unit arrived, and they set the dog loose to sniff around our bikes. It sniffed, and sniffed some more, until it came to a halt next to me. I knew I didn't have any drugs on me, but did Johnny have something on him I was unaware of? Panic set in. "May I please take my helmet off?" I requested, feeling like I was about to pass out.

"Sure, go ahead. Then slowly open your purse hanging from your hip," the police officer replied. I tossed my helmet to the side of the bike, finding immediate relief in my head and neck. But my nerves were still on edge. I felt intimidated by the drug-sniffing dog.

"Could you move your wallet to the side?" the officer asked, as he was looking inside my purse.

"Sure, no problem," I answered. I noticed it faster than he did. I had transferred my medication from its proper prescription pill bottles into a compact. It was easier to carry them this way instead of lugging around three different bottles. The thought of being out of town without my migraine medication turned me into an anxious wreck, waiting for a migraine to strike.

"What's that? A make-up compact?" the police officer inquired. I glanced up at him, relieved that he seemed to think it was makeup.

"Open it," he ordered. *Oh no!* I thought as his expression changed upon seeing the array of pills inside the compact. I respectfully explained what they were and assured him he already had my license, which he could use to verify my prescription with the pharmacy. Perhaps he suspected he might find a larger stash on one of the other guys. Regardless, he didn't pursue the matter with me any further. Thank you, Jesus!

Out of all the people present, I was the only one carrying any kind of drug. Go figure. The police officers thanked Johnny for his patience and respect and advised him to slow down. After what felt like an eternity on the side of the road, they allowed us to continue our journey without issuing any tickets. I'm fairly certain they wanted Johnny to be aware of their presence and hopefully deter any inappropriate behavior from the MC.

THE BEGINNING OF THE END

I quietly slipped into the bathroom at the reception, eager to change out of my beautiful dress and into my biker costume. With no time to spare, I hadn't been able to stop at home. The fear of missing out gnawed at me, and I was desperate to keep a watchful eye on Johnny. Something felt off, and I couldn't ignore it anymore.

Parking at the back of the clubhouse, I made my way towards the group of people gathered around the blazing fire. It was heartwarming to catch up with friends who had driven in from all over the country. After exchanging a few more hugs, I set off towards the clubhouse, determined to find my husband in the midst of bikers that are basically in the same attire. Spotting him among the crowd, I tapped his shoulder and greeted him with a smile.

"Hey, Honey," I said, hoping for a warm reception.

"Oh, hi. How was the wedding?" he asked, his tone lacking enthusiasm.

"It was good. I wish you could have been there with me," I replied, longing for his presence by my side.

"Don't start," he retorted, visibly annoyed. I knew he was reminding me of the club rule against talking back or arguing in front of his brothers. Despite being well aware of my feelings about it, he seemed indifferent. I kissed him on the cheek and went back outside, settling in a chair by the fire. The tension in my neck was unbearable, and a throbbing headache took hold. Trying to relax in the beauty of the summer night, I gazed up at the clear sky adorned with countless shimmering stars. Suddenly, a voice from behind interrupted my thoughts.

"Wanna drink?" Tammy asked.

"No thanks, I'm good," I replied, declining her offer.

She settled on the stool next to me. "What's going on, Deb? Are you okay? Did you just get here?" She was a club sister; someone I had been trying to distance myself from for some time. I cared about her, but her serious addictions were something I couldn't seem to help her with, and honestly, didn't want to deal with anymore. She realized something was troubling me, and she was concerned.

"I don't know. There's something off about Johnny, and I can't put my finger on it. He's just not himself lately," I confided in her.

She nodded understandingly, her head lowered. Then she asked me if I had talked to my old man about the situation involving Jennifer earlier that day. I had no clue what she was referring to. Jennifer was a close friend of mine, always eager to hang out with bikers. She would do practically anything to have an old man in the club, and I mean anything. She took care of household chores, cooked, cleaned, and... well, you can use your imagination for the rest.

"No," I answered, bewildered. I hadn't heard anything. "Why? What happened?" I inquired; curiosity piqued.

"Well, remember that guy named Ink from the Chicago chapter? The one with 666 tatted on his forehead?" she asked.

"Yeah, I know who you're talking about," I acknowledged, my mind racing with possibilities.

She told me, "He offered to take Jennifer for a ride this afternoon. I guess they went to a bar, had a few drinks, and pulled over on their way back to the party to have sex in the woods." I waited eagerly, expecting her to reveal the significant issue.

"Okay. So?" I prodded. "It's not like that's never happened before."

She sighed and clarified, "Well, Jennifer is pretty upset about it."

"Why?" I asked, a mix of emotions swirling within me. Was it because she had a boyfriend? Or because Ink had the number 666 tattooed on his face, symbolizing his apparent affiliation with Satan? Or perhaps Jennifer didn't want it to happen in the first place?

She shrugged her shoulders and replied, "I don't know."

The tension in my neck tightened even more, and my voice grew louder. "Did she not want this to happen?" I asked once again, seething with anger. I couldn't believe what I was hearing. Yes, this woman had been involved with several of the brothers before, but it was always her choice. Was this encounter against her will? I was ready to unleash my fury. I was ready for war.

The backdoor to the clubhouse was just closing when I put my foot in front of it to walk in. I stormed past the guard at the door, desperately searching for Johnny. Where was he? I checked the kitchen, the bar area, but he was nowhere to be found. Since I wasn't allowed upstairs, I didn't bother. I didn't think he would be up there, anyway. I stood by the front door, waiting for the club guard to open it for me. Remember, non-members like me weren't allowed to touch the doors.

"Open it. Now!" I demanded; my voice raised. I'd reached my breaking point with this club, its suffocating rules, its brothers, and all the nonsense that came with it. The club guard shot me a dirty look but reluctantly opened the door. And there was my husband, sitting on the porch rail, engrossed in conversation and laughter with his brothers.

"You!" I pointed a finger in his face, my anger obvious. "What happened with Jennifer, and when were you planning on telling me about it?"

"What are you talking about, Deb?" Johnny responded, his tone carrying irritation and impatience, but his expression betraying genuine concern.

"You know damn well what I'm talking about. Did Ink rape her?" I confronted him, my accusation sharp and direct. Johnny's brothers continued to stare at me in disbelief. They couldn't believe I would talk to my old man with little to no respect.

"No! What's wrong with you? Where is this coming from?" Johnny retorted, standing firm in defense of his brother. "She wanted it. She was all over him all day," he stated resolutely. I knew Johnny would never allow anything to harm Jennifer. We had all been friends long before joining this club, and I was certain that Johnny would never tolerate such behavior. "Deb, you have to calm down," he pleaded.

"Calm down? Don't tell me to calm down," I snapped back. "I'm out. I'm going home. I'm taking Jennifer and Tammy with me. They're both drunk and acting like idiots. I've had enough. Call me later," I declared, storming off the porch and making my way back to the fire pit to find Tammy. She was in a frenzy, screaming at her old man because he refused to give her another Vicodin. She was coming down from her high, and that was never a good thing. In a fit of anger, he threw a pill at her face. It bounced off her nose and nearly landed in the fire. She scrambled to retrieve it from the ashes and dirt while her old man walked away, indifferent to her distress.

Jennifer sat in a chair by the fire, gently rocking back and forth, lost in a haze of emotions. My heart ached for her as I approached, understanding that she was caught in an ugly situation. With genuine empathy, I urged both Jennifer and Tammy to get in my car. I realized they both needed to leave, given the overwhelming circumstances. The clubhouse was brimming with too many higher-ranking MC members, and I couldn't bear to leave them in their intoxicated, vulnerable, and erratic state of mind they were both in.

THE DRIVE HOME

The car grew eerily quiet, filled only with a sense of anticipation. Tammy sat in the front seat, and Jennifer leaned forward from the back, as if compelled to share a secret. Feeling their distress, I anxiously urged them to tell me what was bothering them.

Tammy, with a look of understanding on her face, hesitated, knowing that her revelation could permanently alter our friendship.

"What is it?" I asked, my voice tinged with both curiosity and concern.

Tammy's gaze remained fixed ahead, and she faltered, teetering on the edge of telling me. "No, I can't tell you. Forget it. It's fine," she murmured, almost retracting her words.

Feeling a surge of frustration, I abruptly pulled the car over to the side of the road, realizing we still had a considerable distance to go before reaching home. "Get out," I uttered sternly, my tone leaving no room for negotiation. They recognized the seriousness in my voice.

"Deb, please stop! Okay, I'll tell you," Tammy finally relented. Jennifer, leaning forward in an attempt to calm my anger, echoed Tammy's plea. Yet, I was seething, unable to comprehend what could unfold now.

And then Jennifer spoke, her words laden with a mix of compassion and concern. "We genuinely think you're a kind person. You're always trying to help everyone else in their time of need. But you have no idea what's happening. We believe it's only fair that we tell you the truth."

"For the love of God, what is it?" I screamed, my emotions unraveling, desperate for answers.

"Your old man is using coke," Tammy blurted out, and just like that, my world shattered into a million pieces.

I couldn't believe it. Johnny promised me he'd never touch drugs again. We'd talked about this when we got married, and I made it clear that there would be serious consequences if he ever used again. I thought he understood. I thought he knew how much was at stake. He would remind me about his recovering brothers in the club and how they stayed clean, trying to convince me of his own sobriety the few times I may have doubted him. But now, it felt like everything was crashing down.

As I kept driving, Tammy and Jennifer shared more details, one after another. It was all too much for me to process. How did I not know any of this? I felt so stupid and betrayed.

I dropped Tammy off first, trying to stay calm so they would keep talking. Jennifer moved to the front seat, and we drove in silence. When we stopped in front of her house, she continued to tell me more, describing the amount of cocaine she had seen. It made me sick to my stomach. How did I not know this? My heart raced, and my hands grew sweaty. Jennifer was in tears by the time I pulled away.

"I love you, Debbie," she said through her sobs. "I had to tell you the truth, no matter what it does to our friendship. You deserved to know."

In that moment, I felt an overwhelming gratitude for their courage. It was an enormous risk for Tammy, especially as a club sister. We were always told to keep the brothers' business secret, never to talk about it with anyone, especially their old ladies. But Tammy broke that rule for me, to make sure I knew the truth.

I'd never felt so broken in my life! The person I loved the most let me down, and it hurt more than I could bear.

Chapter Thirteen

God's Saving Grace

"But God shows his love for us in that while we were still sinners, Christ died for us." ~ Romans 5:8 (ESV)

YOU KNOW YOU HAVE truly remarkable friends when you can reach out to them at three in the morning, and they respond with unwavering love and genuine concern instead of frustration or irritation. I dialed the phone and started crying immediately. I could hear the weariness in her voice, yet she greeted me with tenderness, asking, "Deb, what's wrong?" Stacey, my best friend, has been by my side through thick and thin. From standing beside us on our wedding day to the adventures we shared as kids, she has always been my loyal companion. I find solace in knowing that I can rely on her unconditionally, no matter the circumstances.

My voice was but a whisper. I poured my heart out over the phone, confessing, "I'm so lost. I don't know what to do." Tears streamed down my cheeks as I hastily tossed clothes into a suitcase.

"I feel so stupid. How could I have missed what was going on? How could I be so dumb? What should I do now?"

In an attempt to provide comfort, my dear friend offered words of reassurance, saying, "Everything will be alright. I'm sorry, Deb. Try to get some rest."

But sleep was out of the question. The thought of being home when Johnny returned in the morning was unbearable. I needed time to process this overwhelming situation, even though I didn't know how to navigate through it. Being inside my own house felt suffocating, prompting an intense desire to escape.

"Don't worry about me. I'll find a hotel room and stay there," I assured her.

"Keep me posted once you get a room," she replied with concern.

Gathering my small, five-pound dog and fighting with the weight of my suitcase, which seemed to grow heavier with every step, I quickly departed from my house. I ventured to several hotels in town, only to be met with the disappointing reality that none allowed pets. The clerk at the last hotel appeared tempted to bend the rules, observing my swollen, teary eyes, but ultimately, she adhered to the policy.

"I apologize, but we have a no-pets policy. I can't jeopardize my job," she explained. She inquired about my well-being, asking if I needed her to call the police, if someone had harmed me.

If only she knew. "It's alright. Honestly, I'll manage," I muttered. I lowered my head and walked back to my car, overwhelmed with a mix of emotions.

Maybe flying somewhere would provide some rest. With that thought in mind, I drove to the airport and parked my car. The parking lot wasn't a huge one, but I parked as far away from the terminal as possible. I needed a moment to gather my thoughts. Reclining the driver's seat back, I held my small dog close and prayed. I needed sleep, yet it eluded me. Instead, a concern crept in—I worried that leaving my car running for too long might draw attention and unwanted interactions. Reluctantly, I left the airport behind. I knew it wasn't feasible to fly anywhere.

Another idea sparked in my mind—I could chill out for a moment at the church. No one would be there at this hour. I was seeking refuge, a sense of peace that I'd recently associated with the church. Yearning for that tranquility, I parked my car at the rear of the church, in the far reaches of the parking lot. With the same hope of finding sleep as I did at the airport, I waited, prayed, and wept. But my racing mind overwhelmed me, making sleep an impossibility. I needed time to process everything. I didn't want to go back home, I couldn't sleep. So, I kept driving. Along the way, I stopped at a gas station to stock up on coffee and energy drinks to keep me going.

The sun began to rise. I found myself in a Walmart parking lot in a small city beyond my home. It had been a few hours of relentless driving. I pleaded with God, desperately seeking answers. "Why?" I cried. "Why, God? What am I supposed to do?" I reminded Him of the conversation Johnny and I had at the start of our relationship—the ultimatum I had set regarding drug use. If I ever caught him using drugs, it would mark the end of our marriage. Devastation consumed me, as I felt like this might be the end. I was overwhelmed with heartbreak.

Once again, I parked toward the back of the parking lot, mirroring my previous stops at the airport and the church, in search of some sleep. Except the sun was now fully up, and the caffeine from multiple cups of coffee and energy drinks coursed through my veins. I jumped in the back seat, nestled with my dog, covering us with my coat to block out any lingering light. Finally, sleep found me, if only for a couple of hours. I woke up to the persistent ringing of my phone. It took me a moment to register my surroundings and recall the events of the past day. Memories rushed back, flooding my consciousness. My phone continued to ring incessantly. Struggling among the chaos of coffee cups and blankets, I fumbled to locate it. The ringing momentarily ceased, only to start again. Finally, stretching over the center console, just as Jennifer had done the previous night, I managed to find my phone. It was Johnny. He had bombarded my phone with texts earlier, which went unnoticed. Did he know? I wondered if Tammy confided in her old man about her confession to me. If so, he would have undoubtedly informed Johnny. I wasn't ready to face him just yet. I had some things to take care of first. I threw my phone in the back seat without responding.

Before entering Walmart, I caught a glimpse of my disheveled appearance in the rearview mirror. I looked worn out, mascara smudging my face with black streaks. My false lashes fell from my eyes and settled onto my cheeks. I plucked them off and attempted to wipe away the streaks with spit on my finger as best I could. My hair stood in disarray, defying gravity in every direction. But I couldn't bring myself to care. I walked towards the pharmacy department in Walmart. I noticed a few passing strangers casting side glances at my disheveled state, but their opinions mattered little to me in that moment.

"Excuse me," I approached the clerk behind the glass window, mustering up what little strength I had left. "I'm looking for a drug test." I could see the judgment in her eyes as she glanced at my appearance, and she responded with a dismissive roll of her eyes, pointing me toward the tests. Little did I know how many types of drug tests existed. It took some time, but I narrowed down the specific one I needed. After paying for it, I returned to my car, tossing the test onto the back seat, next to my phone, and resumed my journey on the road to nowhere.

I had no desire to go home. With my phone turned off, I decided to drive towards the shoreline of Lake Superior. Stepping out of the car, I walked over to a park bench and positioned myself perfectly to watch the mighty waves crashing against the rocks just before me. It was as if nature mirrored the impending storm that was about to unleash in my own life. The rhythmic motion of the waves held me captive, drawing me into a trance-like state. Lost in my thoughts, contemplating the approaching waves that would soon disrupt my world, a man approached me, interrupting my thoughts to inform me that dogs were not allowed in this area of the park. "How kind of you to let me know," I said with a sarcastic tone. It was precisely the outlet I needed to unleash the anger I felt towards Johnny and the MC.

I snapped back, my voice filled with rage, "Are you kidding me? My dog weighs a mere five pounds and hasn't left my lap. Do I look like I give a damn? Mind your own business, or I'll make sure to mind it for you." I must have appeared like a madwoman, and my words certainly matched the sentiment. He quickly lowered his head and retreated to wherever he came from.

Caught in a peculiar predicament, I struggled with what I was supposed to do. I was hesitant to confide in my family members, fearing the embarrassment that would accompany sharing my situation. I didn't want to reach out to my newfound friends from the church, afraid of the potential judgment that might await me. Although I had surrounded myself with individuals whom I believed were my friends from the club, I soon realized I couldn't reach out to them either.

If it weren't for my relationship with God, I would have felt overwhelmingly alone during this time. Yet, I knew deep within that

PROPERTY OF THE KING

He was by my side, steadfast and unfailing. I leaned into Him, seeking wisdom and strength from the One who would never abandon me.

I grabbed my phone from my pocket, intending to call a dear friend whom I've known for years. Friends like him are like the stars in the night sky—always present, even if not always visible. With my phone on, I glanced down at the screen, only to be greeted by a flood of missed calls and texts from Johnny. It was a rarity for me to be unavailable to him, and I could only imagine his growing concern. Disregarding the crazy number of notifications, I found my friend's contact and called him.

"Hey, I'm in a bit of a situation and not sure where to turn or what to do. I'm in Marquette with my dog." Knowing he spent a lot of time in Marquette, I asked him if he knew of any dog-friendly places to stay, my voice carrying the weight of uncertainty. I could sense the genuine concern in his response. "Deb, come back here. Stay at my house. You can park your car in the garage, and nobody will suspect a thing."

"Are you sure?" I questioned, seeking reassurance. His answer came without hesitation. "Absolutely. Should I come and get you? I'm worried about you driving all the way back home."

"No, I'm pretty exhausted, but I think I can manage the drive to your place," I replied, aware of my tired state. Along the journey, I'd pull over a few times to rest my eyes and steal fleeting moments of sleep. Exhaustion consumed me entirely, leaving my body void of the adrenaline and caffeine that had fueled me earlier. During the drive, my friend checked in on me multiple times, making sure I was okay.

I pulled into the garage of his house and was greeted by his daughters. The girls eagerly took care of my dog, while their father directed me downstairs to the welcoming embrace of the spare bedroom. "The girls and I got it all ready for you," he assured me.

Climbing into bed, I couldn't help but feel grateful for my friend's thoughtfulness. Aware of my apprehension regarding Johnny's incessant phone calls, he had already set up a phone charger and placed a glass of ice water on the nightstand. Finally, the comforting embrace of sleep enveloped me, offering rest from the whirlwind of emotions that consumed me.

When I woke up, a sense of resolution washed over me, bringing with it the realization that I could no longer run from the inevitable. It was time to confront Johnny and the harsh reality I'd been trying to escape. With a determined sigh, I reached over the pillows for my phone, unplugging it from the charger, and dialed his number, bracing myself for the difficult conversation at hand.

THE STORM AT HAND

"Where the hell are you?" he asked, his voice tinged with panic.

"That's not your concern," I replied sharply, my frustration obvious.

"Don't give me that. You're my wife. What the hell is going on, Deb?" he demanded, his desperation seeping through the phone. Did he truly not know? It had been hours since my disappearance, and I was certain he had conducted his own investigations during my silence. Deep down, he must have had some inkling of what he was in for.

"Just come home," he pleaded, his voice wavering between frustration and concern.

I expressed my heartfelt gratitude to my dear friend for providing me refuge during this trying time. He had been remarkably understanding, never prying into my situation. With kindness and compassion, he ensured my safety and readiness to return home. Giving him a warm hug and a sincere thank you, I said goodbye.

As I headed home, I started in prayer again. I needed to gather my strength, for I felt defeated even before reaching my house. I knew Johnny would attempt to deny the accusations of drug use that had been leveled against him by my friends the previous night. I refused to be swayed by his manipulative excuses and lies. Undoubtedly, he had spent hours crafting a web of justifications during my absence. However, this time, I was prepared. I'd consulted a friend who was a pharmacist and asked if it was possible to test positive for cocaine without consuming it.

"No, Debbie. To test positive, he would have had to ingest the drug and have it in his system," she assured me firmly.

"Thank you for clearing this up," I said, my gratitude seeping into my voice.

With newfound strength, I stepped through the front door, ready to confront Johnny. My emotions churned within me—a storm of disappointment, anger, and resignation. Deep down, I knew he loved me and was genuinely worried about my well-being during my unresponsive state. The traces of panic in his voice earlier were impossible to ignore.

"What's happening, Deb?" he inquired, his tone veering between innocence and ignorance.

"You know exactly what's happening," I whispered, my voice laden with disappointment and a touch of sorrow.

"Deb, Tammy is an addict. You can't believe anything she says," Johnny protested, trying to cast doubt on the credibility of my friends. I couldn't help but wonder about the conversations he must have had with his brothers in the club during my absence.

He knew the truth. He adamantly swore that both women were lying. Fueled by anger and frustration, I threw the drug test at him and declared, "Well, you won't mind taking the test then."

His head tilted to the side, a confused expression crossing his face as he asked, "Test? You bought a drug test?"

"You bet I did. And I'll watch you pee on the stick for good measure," I retorted, determination seeping into my voice.

"Deb, come on," he pleaded, attempting to dissuade me.

"Do it, or I'm gone!" I yelled, tears streaming down my face. But these tears were no longer born out of sadness; they were a manifestation of the seething rage within me.

"Fine, I'll take it. But I want you to know that it'll probably come up positive," he admitted, his voice filled with resignation.

Here we go, I thought to myself, ready to expose the truth.

He began weaving a story, claiming that someone had been doing a line of cocaine on the bar and he accidentally leaned into it.

I looked at him, a smile playing on my lips. I'd been waiting for this. He was desperately grasping at lies, hoping that I would change my mind or believe him to avoid taking the test. I couldn't deny that I might have done the same if our roles were reversed. He knew our marriage hung in the balance. He knew the impending storm and was desperate to find an escape. But it was too late. The drug test, like a pregnancy test, would reveal two lines if it was positive and one line if it was negative.

We anxiously waited for a few minutes; the tension in the air was thick.

The results appeared before us—two lines, confirming a positive result.

"Deb," he stammered, his voice laced with fear. "I'm sorry."

"Just be honest. Stop lying and tell me the truth," I pleaded, my voice filled with a mix of pain and desperation. We both found ourselves seated at the kitchen counter. "Please, just tell me the truth. I deserve that," I implored, my heart aching for transparency.

He hung his head low, his voice filled with shame as he confessed, "Deb, I used it last night. It was a one-time thing."

Devastation washed over me once again, and my body trembled uncontrollably. He reached out and held me, and as much as I resisted, I needed his touch. It felt strange to be filled with such anger and yet yearn for the safety of his embrace. He had always been my protector, my rock. In the darkest moments of my life, he'd never instilled fear within me. But now, trust shattered, I couldn't believe his claim of a single slip-up. It hardly mattered anymore. He broke that trust, and I knew deep down that I could never trust him to be or remain sober, especially within the confines of the MC.

My head throbbed with the weight of it all, and exhaustion consumed me. Johnny tucked me into bed as he grappled with the gravity of the situation himself.

When I woke, I mustered the strength to recount the conversation I had with Tammy and Jennifer on the way home. Johnny was furious that they shared so much information with me. He insisted on talking to Tammy himself, so I dialed her number. As expected, she didn't answer. It was no surprise. She made it clear the night before that we would never speak again.

Next, I called Jennifer, hopeful that she would confirm the things she said during our ride home from the clubhouse. I put the phone on speaker so Johnny could hear our conversation, confident that she would confess to her earlier statements. But her response shocked me.

"What? I didn't say that. I don't remember what I said. I drank too much," Jennifer claimed, denying everything. I couldn't believe my ears. I repeated our conversation, growing angrier by the second. Yet, she continued to deny any knowledge of it. She admitted to doing a line of cocaine with a club member, but refused to admit anything further. That friendship, too, came to an abrupt end.

I was dumbfounded, shaking my head as I relayed the situation to Johnny. Both Tammy and Jennifer were lying, trying to protect themselves. They knew that being labeled as rats was the worst thing you could do within the MC. Neither of them would ever be welcome at the clubhouse again.

In the end, I didn't need their admission to validate the conversation we had. I knew what I heard, and their lies only solidified my belief in its truth. Besides, Johnny already confessed, although not to the entire truth—I doubted I would ever know the whole truth, and perhaps I didn't need to. Deception is deception.

Now that the truth was out in the open, the question loomed before us: Where do we go from here? I loved my husband, and I knew he loved me. My pride urged me to leave him, insisting that I didn't deserve this. But I recognized that pride was a delusion, filled with spite and bitterness. It declared, "I don't want God to be God. I want to be God!" I could have chosen the path of self-righteousness, but deep down, I knew I had to extend grace, for I knew of the grace that God had extended to me. Alone, I couldn't navigate through this mess; I needed the strength that only God could provide. I wanted to forgive my husband, but how?

Chapter Fourteen
Forgiveness Is a Beautiful Thing

"Be kind to one another, tenderhearted, forgiving one another, as God in Christ forgave you." ~ Ephesians 4:32 (ESV)

PSYCHOLOGISTS DEFINE FORGIVENESS AS a conscious, deliberate decision to release feelings of resentment or vengeance toward a person or group who has harmed you, regardless of whether they deserve your forgiveness.

"For if you forgive others their trespasses, your heavenly Father will also forgive you, but if you do not forgive others their trespasses, neither will your Father forgive your trespasses." (Matthew 6:14-15 ESV)

I understood that forgiving John was not only crucial for the restoration of our marriage, but also aligned with my Christian faith. Yet I grappled with the practicality of forgiveness. It's relatively easier to forgive someone you don't know well or whose offense was minor, as you can easily move on without having to confront the pain they caused. Yet forgiving someone you deeply love for betraying you was an entirely different challenge for me. I often wondered how other women could find it in their hearts to forgive their cheating husbands and rebuild trust. While the offense John committed was not infidelity, it would require a similar level of grace and forgiveness to move forward and regain trust in our relationship.

This is where the importance of the church community became clear. It wasn't merely about attending a physical building to fulfill an obligation. Rather, it was about the relationships formed while being in communion with the Lord and fellow believers. I needed the support and guidance of my sisters and brothers in Christ to help me navigate this difficult journey. Left to my own devices, I might have eventually forgiven John, but not without making him suffer and pay dearly for a prolonged period of time.

WHERE DO I START

I reached out to my pastor and asked if I could stop by for some advice. He and his wife welcomed me warmly, mentioning that their children would love to see me. Though I wasn't in the mood for playful interactions, I realized that engaging in innocent fun was exactly what I needed. I spent a few minutes wrestling with their kids. Their laughter filled the room. Eventually, he suggested we sit on the front porch to talk. His wife took the baby from my hands and began tickling him as she walked into the kitchen.

My pastor and I settled down on the porch, overlooking a breathtaking field of wildflowers. I opened up and shared everything, confessing my sins and recounting the entire story. There is something powerful about confessing to another human being. While I feared judgment, once I started speaking, there was no stopping me. My pastor listened with compassion, his face displaying genuine concern as tears once again streamed down my face. I was so tired of crying. I shared the details of that harrowing night, from beginning to end. He told me I could call him or his wife if I ever needed a place of refuge again.

"It wasn't just about needing a place to go," I explained. I could have hidden out at my parents', cousins', aunts', or friends' houses. Shame held me back. I didn't want to hear the words, "I told you so, Debbie. What did you expect, hanging out with people like that?" I didn't want my loved ones to worry about me. I had always been seen as a strong woman who could handle anything, but this time, I felt utterly broken.

"Are you considering leaving him, Deb?" my pastor asked. I admitted that the thought had crossed my mind. I no longer trusted John, but deep down, I didn't want to leave him. Every fiber of my being knew this. Divorce was not an option on the table. I loved him wholeheartedly, and I understood that love didn't always resemble the idealized stories portrayed on social media. I was determined to fight for my marriage. I realized that if I walked away, John would only spiral further into the dark hole he was trapped in, and who knows what could happen. He couldn't see it because he was deeply entangled in it. Over the past year, the Lord had been working in my life, allowing me to see the evil in the club life that John couldn't.

I recognized that John's path was not my responsibility, and I couldn't be his Holy Spirit. Only God could work in his heart. However, my love for him compelled me to help him through this journey. I had no idea how much stronger our marriage would become because of this struggle. Seeking guidance, I asked my pastor what I should do. He advised me to pray and seek guidance in the Word. He suggested I take time to process everything and return to talk to him. He also proposed that both of us attend marriage counseling at the church.

It was a starting point, but I still didn't know how I could forgive him. Despite my love for him, anger still simmered within me. I needed the Holy Spirit to assist me in working through these emotions. If I followed the advice of the secular world, they would tell me to leave, pack my bags, and go. They would question how I could ever trust him again and argue that I deserved better. But my Christian friends reminded me of my identity in Christ. I had been forgiven, and that same forgiveness granted me the strength and courage to extend forgiveness to others. Especially my husband.

I realized forgiving John might be the easier part of our situation. Rebuilding trust in our relationship would be the true challenge. It would require effort from both of us and a willingness to work on our marriage. I expressed my gratitude to my pastor and his wife for their time and kind words. I left their house feeling encouraged and hopeful.

In times of struggle, we all seek outlets to help us cope. Some may turn to drugs or alcohol, while others resort to food, exercise, or maybe even impulsive shopping. Although I felt the temptation to drown my sorrows in some of those avenues, I knew the joy from any one of these things would be fleeting. I turned to people who would support me through these difficult times, speaking truth into my life while praying for me.

DEBORAH MCKINZIE

A PLACE WHERE I ALWAYS FIND PEACE

Filled with a deep longing for guidance, I laced up my running shoes and embarked on my favorite trail. This was a place where I had previously had great conversations with God, and I hoped to hear from Him again.

As I ran, my heart poured out its questions: "What am I supposed to do? I'm so sad." I screamed these words aloud, as if God were running alongside me. Mile after mile, I pushed myself harder and faster, climbing the steep mountain with determination. Sweat and tears poured down my face, exhaustion crept in. I had never felt so utterly lost.

And then, I heard it. Clear and unmistakable: "LOVE HIM!"

"What?" I asked in disbelief.

Again, the voice echoed within me, not audibly but resounding in my heart: "LOVE HIM."

God's message pierced through my pain, reminding me of the immense love He had for me. A love so powerful that He gave His only Son, so that whoever believes in Him shall not perish but have eternal life. In that moment, I realized that walking in the footsteps of Christ meant extending forgiveness and love to my husband. It required humbling myself. Walking away would have been easy, and many would have understood my decision. But staying and loving him through this was what I had to do.

After all, I had threatened divorce in the past over far less. But things changed. The Holy Spirit filled me, and He was prompting me to love and forgive. Even though I felt like a fool, I knew this was the path I had to take. While running, I engaged in an internal conversation with

God, and it was as if He pressed a button, causing my own sins to flash before my eyes. Running through the dense forest, I yelled, "I get it! I get it! I too am a sinner!" It was the perfect time to look at my own sin in all of this. Let's face it, I was going along with everything, even if I didn't know about the drugs.

My perspective shifted, and I returned from that run a different person, fueled by newfound strength and wisdom.

Upon my return, I asked John if we could sit down and talk. I made it clear that I couldn't tell him to leave the motorcycle club, but I could establish boundaries. I vowed never to step foot in a clubhouse again and severed all ties with the MC. Although I felt a sense of loss for some relationships I had within the club, I knew that true understanding of why I left would only come when others experienced the transformative power of the Holy Spirit, as I did. While I would miss them and would continue praying for them, I discarded everything associated with the club, returning the vest that symbolized ownership of John and the MC. I declared that no club member was welcome on our property, and I would involve the police if necessary. I also shared my fears about the direction of our marriage if he remained in the club. However, I recognized that the decision was his alone to make.

The trust between us was shattered, and anxiety accompanied me every time he rode his bike with the club. I explained I wouldn't passively wait at home while he went away on weekends. Instead, I would become more involved in the church and make efforts to visit out-of-town friends. The distance and diverging paths frightened me, but I held onto faith in the Lord, trusting that He would work everything out. I didn't know the how, but my hope in God was enough. When I couldn't trust my husband, I placed my trust in God.

John agreed to respect the boundaries I'd set and expressed his need for time to contemplate his choices. He wasn't prepared to leave the club just yet, and I understood his hesitation. If he left immediately, he would always feel a sense of longing. He genuinely believed that these men were his friends, his family, and he loved them, believing that they loved him in return.

Recognizing the importance of giving him space to think about our future, I decided to create some distance between us. Stacey, who'd been supportive throughout these struggles, suggested that I spend the weekend at her house. It was exactly what I needed. God has a way of providing people and opportunities in our lives to help us through challenging times. Although leaving John behind saddened me, I understood that we both needed this time apart to find clarity. I jumped on a plane and headed for Ohio.

While I was away, John was expected to attend a "mandatory" bike rally out of town with the motorcycle club. I fully expected him to go, so I was surprised when I saw his name appear on my phone. Did something happen? Excusing myself from the table, I took the call. He asked how things were going and what I was up to. I shared with him the details of the massage Stacey treated me to and the beautiful restaurant where we were dining. She has always spoiled me rotten. (Everyone should have a friend like her). The meal was wonderful, and it was great to catch up with her and her friends. I almost forgot about the drama I left behind. I could sense the happiness in John's voice, because I was able to get away and relax.

Curious about his whereabouts, I asked, "Where are you?" He responded, "At home." I couldn't believe it. "At home? Weren't you supposed to be at the rally?" I inquired.

John explained that he'd been thinking a lot about our conversation and didn't want me to be upset every time he attended club events. He shared that he'd taken a ride alone during the day to clear his head. I smiled at the similarity of our actions. I go for a run; he goes for a ride.

Concerned about him potentially getting in trouble for not attending the rally, I asked, "Aren't you worried about the consequences of missing the event?" He simply replied, "Maybe."

Before leaving my dear friend, I embraced her tightly and expressed my gratitude for her unwavering support during this difficult time. When I boarded the flight back home, I had the opportunity to reflect on everything that had unfolded over the weekend. My heart overflowed with love and thankfulness.

Throughout all the wondering and worrying about how John would come to see the truth or if our marriage would survive, God had a plan. Even through our suffering, God remained good. There are few things the devil hates more than a Christian marriage. He attempted to tempt both of us, hoping I would refuse to forgive John and believing he could continue tempting John with the allure and lifestyle of the MC. The devil seeks to kill and destroy anything good that can only come from God. It almost worked, but our God is greater than the evil and darkness of Satan's ways.

God says to trust in the Lord with all your heart and lean not on your own understanding. In all your ways acknowledge Him, and He will make your paths straight. (Proverbs 3:5-6 NIV)

Indeed, God's redeeming love pursued both John and me relentlessly. Despite the chaotic and raging nature of our story, God extended His forgiveness when we turned to Him in repentance. He was actively working to transform our lives and restore our marriage. What Satan aimed to destroy and annihilate, God redeemed and brought new life to. His love and grace have the power to overcome the darkest moments in our lives. He breathed hope into our brokenness. We were witnesses to the miraculous workings of God's power in our lives and, most importantly, in our marriage.

During this time, John's struggle with the decision of leaving the club continued. He found himself in a difficult position, wanting to make me happy while also grappling with the desire to please his brothers in the motorcycle club. It was a confusing and challenging period for him, and it persisted for months.

Despite the ongoing struggle, I remained obedient to the Lord's command to love him unconditionally. I tried to love him with the same fervor and compassion that Jesus would have shown him. This was no simple task.

Meanwhile, John worked diligently to fulfill the requirements of his probationary period, hoping to regain his previous position as the boss of the club. Because of his absence at the MC party, he faced club discipline. He went from being the boss to being a probate. The thirty-day probation stretched out before him, and he eagerly waited for it to end.

His physical health took a turn for the worse during his probation. His hip started causing him significant pain, making it difficult for him to ride his bike for extended periods. Despite the pain, he pushed himself to meet the demands placed on him by the club, enduring criticism and bullying from his brothers. I vividly remember the day he returned home from an event, visibly distraught and struggling to dismount his bike. The pain had become unbearable.

In search of relief, John scheduled a doctor's appointment, which ultimately led to the discovery that he needed a hip replacement. This prognosis meant that he would be unable to ride his bike for an extended period, and it also brought an end to the mistreatment he had endured within the club while he was a probate. The physical ailment became a turning point in his journey, as God slowly began unveiling the truth to John.

It was a remarkable and beautiful process to witness. The scales started falling from his eyes, and prayers that had been earnestly offered were being answered. Although John's spiritual vision remained clouded by his sin and the false identity he derived from the club, it provided me with clarity about what I needed to pray for. The transformation and revelation taking place in his life were undeniable signs of God's work, and it fueled my determination to continue praying for his spiritual growth and freedom from the MC's influence.

The cold October month arrived, and John made the dreaded decision to schedule his hip replacement surgery. He'd been putting it off for as long as he could, wanting to squeeze in as much riding as his body would allow before the procedure. The snow began to fall in the Upper Peninsula of Michigan, adding a sense of urgency to his desire to ride.

In the middle of all of this, we also sold our house and everything in it a week prior to his surgery. It was a time of significant upheaval, and we scrambled to furnish our new home before the surgery took place. It felt like one challenge after another, but somehow things fell into place.

On the day of the surgery, with snow-covered roads, I drove John to the hospital. As they wheeled him into the surgical room, I experienced a profound love for him like never before. It was a love rooted in God's presence and grace.

The ride back from the hospital was a painful one for John, but after a couple of long days and sleepless nights at the hospital, it was time to make the two-hour trip back home. We both knew that the road to recovery lay ahead, and it would not be easy.

John's recovery progressed well, and I tried to take on the role of a caring nurse. Again, not an easy task.

While a couple of his club brothers called a few times to check on him, the conversations were brief and left him feeling disappointed. He shared his concerns about the club, expressing doubts about whether it was truly what he thought it to be. I felt a mix of happiness and sympathy for him at that moment. It wasn't an easy realization for him, and the struggle was visible on his face. Yet God was continuing to remove the scales from his eyes, revealing more of the truth. Thank you, Jesus!

I posted a picture of John on Facebook snow-blowing our driveway shortly after his surgery. I thought he was crazy. I even offered to do it myself, but he was determined to do it. Little did I know it would upset his brothers in the club so much when they saw my post. He received a phone call minutes after I posted it. "Dude, you can snow-blow your driveway, but you can't make it to the clubhouse for bar night?" said the guy who was holding the position of boss while John was recovering. I can't disclose the rest of the conversation, but it clearly bothered John. They exchanged heated words, and eventually, John ended the call. I didn't probe for details. I believed in God's ability to work things out, and it seemed more scales were falling from John's eyes.

There have been numerous instances in my life where I thought I could control the situations, believing I could make things happen. However, the truth is there are circumstances beyond my control, including this struggle and others I've faced. What I can do is pray, remain humble, and trust in God's timing and plans.

About a week after that conversation, John decided to leave the club. He gathered all his belongings associated with the club, just as I had done months earlier, and made his way up to the clubhouse for the very last time.

All scales were removed from his eyes. Praise the Lord!

Chapter Fifteen

Never Going Back

"Whoever walks with the wise becomes wise, but the companion of fools will suffer harm." ~ Proverbs 13:20 (ESV)

"You're kidding me?" I whispered into the phone. "What? When?" My dad called to deliver the heartbreaking news that our dear friend, Big G, passed away. He'd been battling health issues for a long time, and his fight had come to an end. Big G was truly one of the best guys I had the pleasure of knowing. He was one of John's first friends when he moved to the area.

Big G possessed a gentle soul that touched the hearts of everyone who had the privilege of knowing him. He was a man I held in high regard within the MC world. He was a founding member of the riding club that John initially joined upon moving to the Upper Peninsula of Michigan. John rode alongside Big G for many years before taking the fateful path that led him to stepping up to the MC that nearly drained the life out of him. Despite never fully understanding John's decision to "step up," Big G remained steadfast in his love for John throughout it all.

Big G was the epitome of someone who cherished riding his bike, finding joy in laughter, wearing a contagious smile, and simply savoring the wonders of life.

A few days after learning of his passing, his wife reached out to me via text. "Hi Debbie and John, I want to personally invite you to Big

G's celebration of life on Sept. 24th at noon at the clubhouse. I have spoken to club officers, and you are both welcome to come. We hope to see you there! He loved you guys."

Internal conflict arose within me as I read her message. *"Ugh! Why do they have to hold his celebration of life at the clubhouse?"* I thought. *"Couldn't they have it at the funeral home and then gather at the clubhouse?"* I realized in that moment that I was being selfish. It wasn't about me and my preferences. It was about honoring Big G, celebrating the life he lived, and supporting his family. This event was meant to pay tribute to him, not conform to my personal desires. In fact, if I were still part of the MC world, I could understand how the clubhouse was the perfect setting to commemorate him. He had an immense love for his brothers and his club, which played a significant role in his life.

The news of Big G's passing and the invitation to his celebration of life at the clubhouse stirred conflicting emotions with us. John and I intentionally distanced ourselves from any bike related events or rides since he left the MC. We made a mutual decision to leave our past behind and forge ahead in our lives. The idea of attending anything associated with the MC world made us uneasy, to say the least. We found contentment in being independent riders, free from the trappings of club affiliations.

We attempted a few times to re-engage with people from different clubs, but these encounters proved to be less than positive experiences.

The first instance was at a charity event organized by a MC club to support my cousin, who was battling cancer. I attended alone, as John wasn't ready to be in that kind of environment again, and I respected his decision. I arrived late and left early, and while the overall experience wasn't as dreadful as I had expected, there was something about the leather vests, bandanas, and bikes that triggered memories I desperately wanted to forget. It reminded me of the control I was once under, and it stirred uneasiness within me.

The second occasion was a birthday party for a friend hosted by our buddy Bones, who was an ex-MC member from the same chapter as John. Despite John's reservations, I convinced him it would be just fine since Bones assured us that no one from the former MC chapter would be present. Although John was no longer part of the club and left on good terms, there were still strained relationships between him and some of his former brothers, which is why we didn't want to run into them.

Against John's better judgment, he attended the party to show support and celebrate with our friends. Even during our ride over to the party, he continued to express his reservations. In that moment, I reminded him that these were people who shared the same perspective on club life that we did. It was important for us to be part of their celebration.

I reflected on the teachings of the apostle Paul, who commands the need for believers to work out their own salvation with fear and trembling, as it is God who works in us, enabling us to live according to His good pleasure. I understood that obedience to the Lord and turning away from sin required continual effort, and placing myself in unfavorable settings and surrounding myself with the wrong company hindered my sanctification. I could go from walking with Christ to acting like a gangster really fast. This is exactly why John and I protect our social space at all costs.

PROPERTY OF THE KING

It was our first time visiting Bones's renovated garage, and I couldn't help but admire the impressive display of his carpentry skills and love for motorcycles. The hanging motorcycle above the bar was a captivating sight. John quickly found his spot at the bar, while I joined the birthday girl and her children, who were playing pool. The atmosphere seemed enjoyable and relaxed until an unexpected turn of events unfolded.

The door swung open. I immediately noticed the club patches on the newcomer before my gaze met his face. A sense of dread washed over me, and my eyes instinctively searched for John. "Patch," as he was known, entered the bar with an air of arrogance, accompanied by his wife, who now held the title of old lady. At that moment, I knew we should have left immediately, but against our better judgment, we stayed.

An unsettling feeling gripped me, and sweat soaked my armpits. From across the bar, I watched as Patch sat down next to my husband, pulling something from his newly adorned vest. My mind raced with worries—was it a knife? A gun? Fortunately, it turned out to be just a fancy cigar, perhaps a peace offering of sorts. However, the tension continued to escalate.

Soon enough, Patch's wife detached herself from his side and approached the birthday girl and me. She made it a point to emphasize how proud she was to wear her "Property of" patches on her vest, displaying them as if she were a peacock flaunting its feathers. She definitely wanted to enlighten us about the significance of wearing a club vest.

Unimpressed by her words, I responded harshly, expressing my skepticism, and hoping that she would one day see the truth behind the lies. This did not sit well with her, and she invaded my personal space, clearly showing her displeasure.

In that moment, my composure crumbled, and I unleashed a torrent of profanity that sharply contrasted with the praises I had sung earlier in the day. The worshipful demeanor I had displayed earlier gave way to a more aggressive side as I engaged in a heated confrontation.

She hurried back to her husband, sharing my venomous words with him. He removed the cigar from his mouth, wiped the stream of spit from his chin, and resorted to a derogatory term I hadn't heard in years. "You cunt," he spat. That was the final straw.

Without hesitation, John grabbed him and forcefully pinned him against the wall. The cigar flew, and its ember and ashes grazed my face. Standing over Patch, John vehemently warned him never to speak to his wife like that again. It was as if witnessing the verbal abuse toward me triggered an eruption of pent-up emotions, transforming the emotional turmoil into a physical confrontation.

Bones swiftly intervened, darting out from behind the bar to separate John and Patch. Meanwhile, my mouth continued to run, with my finger pointed firmly in Patch's face, leaving no words unsaid about him and his motorcycle club. There was no holding back on my part. It was one of those rare moments in life when everything turns red, and this was undeniably one of them.

John attempted to push aside barstools in his determination to confront Patch once more, but a moment of clarity prevailed, and the fighting ceased. The club member and his "property" eventually left the party, while John and I lingered a bit longer before bidding our own goodbyes.

PROPERTY OF THE KING

"Oh boy, what a delightful evening that was," I remarked sarcastically to John as we trudged our way home. "Never again will I willingly put us in such a dreaded position. I hate what I become when I'm surrounded by that club. I'm sorry for encouraging you to go."

John remained silent throughout the rest of the night, his mind likely churning with thoughts he decided not to share with me. Probably for the best.

I was getting ready for bed that night and I felt an overwhelming urge to repent for my behavior. Oh God, forgive me, for I have sinned. I remembered the book of James. He had some wise words about the tongue, didn't he? Blessings and curses shouldn't coexist, my dear brothers and sisters. Quite a concept to grasp. Ugh!

I couldn't help but feel remorse for my performance at the birthday bash. It seems this whole incident made me even more protective of my precious social space. After all, if I wanted to be more like Christ, I needed to refrain from acting like a gangster. Oh, how blessed I am that God himself works tirelessly to mold me into a more Christ-like figure. Left to my own devices, I'd surely be doomed.

Weeks later, John caught wind of some delightful rumors. Apparently, he was "put out bad" from the club for daring to disrespect their holy patches during our little escapade. Oh, the horror! Who knew that a simple altercation without proper respect for their sacred symbols could have such dire consequences? My, how times have changed. It seems the criteria for being "put out bad" has expanded beyond shooting up, being a snitch, or being a thief (or perhaps even writing a scandalous book about MC life). These days, it appears any whimsical reason deemed fit by the almighty boss will do. As a result, John now enjoys the privilege of being cut off from his dear brothers and banished from their glorious presence. No more social media friendships or phone calls for him. He's become an outcast, dead to them, erased from their lives.

I hadn't expected having to confront my past affiliation with the club, but life had other plans, didn't it? It all started with the unfortunate passing of Big G. A man of such significance deserved a proper celebration of life, and I knew I had to be there, come what may.

While John couldn't attend, he managed to offer his condolences to Big G's wife when she visited the salon to have her hair done. As for me, there was no way I would miss paying my respects. Big G's wife knew it too, and she reminded me with a meaningful look, asking if she would see me there. How could I disappoint her? I loved her and her husband, and showing my support was the least I could do.

Luckily, my trusty friend and co-worker, Dolly, offered to accompany me to the funeral. She was a friend of Big G and his family as well, and she reassured me she had my back, ready to take on anyone who dared to mess with us. While I didn't foresee any trouble, having her by my side provided a certain comfort in the face of potential awkwardness.

As fate would have it, we hadn't even set foot on the property before I noticed the MC members, remnants of my husband's past, approaching us. I took a quick breath and turned away, but not before catching a brief glimpse of the enforcer's wife. Her nervousness was written all over her face. I empathized with her, remembering the same shoes I once stood in. As for the enforcer himself, he attempted to give me a menacing stare, as if his burly presence alone could intimidate me. Little did he know, I'd long mastered the art of walking past such individuals, pretending they didn't exist. He joined the MC after John's departure, but guilt by association still lingered in my mind. Yet, I refused to waste my energy, positive or negative, on him. I had learned my lesson from the previous encounter at the birthday party. This time, the devil wouldn't claim victory. God taught me I had nothing left to prove.

Dolly, on the other hand, was far from impressed by the enforcer's behavior. His size and title didn't faze her in the slightest. With veins bulging from her neck, she fearlessly confronted him, mockingly suggesting that his eyes might get stuck if he continued with his intense gaze. Dolly, a woman of immense strength both physically and mentally, grew up with antagonistic older brothers who instilled in her the courage to fear no one. I witnessed her confront men before, toe to toe, never backing down. Her presence brought me peace, knowing she would protect me with her life if need be. John was also comforted by knowing she was by my side. We continued to walk toward the clubhouse. Turning to me, she asked, "You okay, Bruh?"

"Yeah, I'm fine. Just planning to act like I do not know who they are," I nonchalantly replied.

"Well, that guy was giving you the death stare, and I didn't appreciate it," she retorted.

"So what? Was he going to push me around in front of all these people?" I shrugged, dismissing any concern. "Whatever. It's done. Let's do this."

Dolly and I made our way to the clubhouse, where a multitude of people had gathered. Bikers and non-bikers mingled at the tables that were set up outside for everyone to sit at. I scanned the area, searching for Big G's wife among the sea of leather. Nothing. The turnout was overwhelming, but not unexpected for a man as remarkable as Big G.

We approached Big G's family to offer our condolences, but his wife was nowhere to be found. Eager to find her as soon as possible, we looked to the clubhouse. I wasn't keen on delving into the lion's den, and Dolly could sense the tension in my body language.

"I'll go in and look for her. Are you going to be alright on your own?" she asked, concern evident in her voice, and on her face.

I couldn't help but laugh at the absurdity of it all. Not long ago, I considered these people my family, my ride or die. They claimed they would do anything for me, just as I would for them. And now, here I was, being asked if I could handle being alone without her by my side.

"Yes, go ahead. I'll be fine," I assured her.

She disappeared briefly before returning, unable to find Big G's wife anywhere. "Want to call it quits and leave?" she suggested.

Part of me wanted to take her up on that offer, to escape the discomfort and intimidation. But I was there for a purpose. I wanted Big G's wife to know that paying my respects and attending the celebration of her husband's life was more important to me than succumbing to any discomfort or intimidation. I was determined to fulfill that mission, to show my gratitude for the life Big G had lived and, furthermore, for the love he always had for John and me. I had no fear that the club, which once embraced me, would harm me. I wouldn't let their negativity taint my purpose.

It felt strange being in a place where almost everyone was instructed to ignore me. So, I was pleasantly surprised when one of my past girlfriends from the club approached me with open arms, exclaiming,

"Come on, girl, give me a hug!" She pulled me into a warm embrace and asked about Johnny, unaware of his absence.

I informed her he couldn't make it because of the club's politics. She simply shrugged and boldly exclaimed, "Screw them," before giving me another tight hug and moving on.

Finally, we spotted her, Big G's wife. Dolly and I made our way to her, circling around the fire pit to show our love and support.

"We've been looking for you," I said, relieved to have found her.

"Oh, you guys, you made it! I'm so happy! Did you grab something to eat? There's plenty of food inside. Are you being treated well?" she asked, her exhaustion apparent.

I didn't want to burden her with the details of my earlier experiences. She deserved peace, not further stress. So, I simply replied, "Yes, everything is good."

After our heartfelt chat, Dolly and I didn't linger much longer. It was time for us to depart. We walked down the driveway, heading back to the car. I turned around for one last glance at the clubhouse and the members assembled there.

At that moment, a realization washed over me like a gentle breeze. It struck me how effortlessly I could blend into the background, unheard and unnoticed. The desperate need to assert my voice dissipated. I no longer craved validation or the need to prove myself. None of it held any significance anymore.

Instead, my heart ached for the people I once called friends. I couldn't harbor any resentment towards them. My expression softened, and empathy flooded my being. I understood them all too well because I had once been one of them. If I were still immersed in that lifestyle, I would have reacted in the same manner they did.

The persona of being the biker bitch, which once defined me, faded away into the past. It no longer encapsulated who I was or who I aspired to be. This gathering served as a powerful reminder of just how far I'd come on my journey of personal growth and transformation by sanctification.

Chapter Sixteen

Living in the Light

"For at one time you were darkness, but now you are light in the Lord. Walk as children of light." ~ Ephesians 5:8 (ESV)

IN THE BOOK OF Romans, "light" refers to moral deeds, and "darkness" to immoral deeds.

"The night is far gone; the day is at hand. So then let us cast off the works of darkness and put on the armor of light. Let us walk properly as in the daytime, not in orgies and drunkenness, not in sexual immorality and sensuality, not in quarreling and jealousy. But put on the Lord Jesus Christ, and make no provision for the flesh, to gratify its desires." (Romans 13:12-14 ESV)

To embrace a life in the light of God, one must first escape the clutches of darkness, and that is not a simple task. Despite John's decision to leave the MC world behind, I understood we would inevitably encounter certain challenges along the way.

AND SO, IT BEGINS....

John had only been out of the club for about a month when I started hearing the rumors.

"I heard you stormed into a bar, causing a scene and going after John," one client eagerly shared while I worked on untangling her wet hair. "And they say you even attacked one of the old ladies at the clubhouse in a fit of rage. I also heard you're the reason John quit the club."

These were just some of the stories she couldn't wait to tell me, hoping to get a reaction. But instead of getting worked up, I couldn't help but laugh. A slight smile crept across my face. How badly I wanted to set the record straight. The old me would have felt the need to defend myself and tear down the person spreading these falsehoods, just to appear superior in the eyes of the gossipers. However, the person I have become, with Christ living in me, no longer feels that urge.

I simply told the woman, "That's not true," and left it at that. She continued with more lies and rumors, attempting to provoke me, but she soon realized her efforts were in vain. This new client, whom I had never worked with before, was likely seeking information to report back to the club. I assured her I didn't care about what anyone said because I knew the truth, and that was all that mattered.

Frustrated, she gave up on the gossip. I finished trimming her hair and never saw her again. The amusing stories circulating in our small town were nowhere near the truth. How could the club ever tell the truth? It seemed beyond their capabilities. It was easier for them to paint John as some kind of villain, weaving dark tales of lies, rather than admitting the simple truth of why he left the MC. Their egos wouldn't allow it.

Some rumors stung a little, but I didn't feel the need to justify them. I couldn't imagine people would believe such things, but looking back, I understood why they did. We had given them reasons to believe these lies through the life we once led. At first, I felt angry with John for putting me in a position where I had to deal with these rumors. Part of me wanted him to pay for it. However, I soon realized that I was as equally responsible as he was. It was a humbling experience to recognize my own contribution to the troubles that came our way.

I no longer cared about what others thought they knew or heard about John or me. That chapter of our lives was over. The truth was that the MC was a dark place, filled with lies that continued to open doors to a demonic realm that I'd witnessed firsthand on more than one occasion. The real enemy was not John or the men in those clubs; it was Satan, the one who seeks to kill and destroy.

These clubs are perpetuating destruction, and it speaks volumes about their nature. They engage in constant battles, seeking to annihilate one another. They fight for territories, power, respect, money, and women. In their world, sex and scandals are considered the norm. Living in this way makes it difficult to discern the truth. You either try to conceal your inner light or extinguish it by succumbing to temptation.

The Bible warns about those who forsake the path of righteousness to walk in darkness, those who rejoice in doing evil and take pleasure in perverseness. They are individuals with crooked paths and deceitful ways (Proverbs 2:13-15 ESV).

The "brothers" in these clubs are living out these verses. I can say this because John and I were once living in the ways of darkness. Our paths were twisted and deceitful. We lied to each other about the sinful world we were immersed in. We attempted to convince our loved ones who wanted us to break free from the MC world that it wasn't as bad as it seemed. We disregarded the severity of our actions. This is precisely what Satan would want us to believe—that it wasn't "that" bad.

WHEN YOU KNOW GOD, YOU KNOW TRUTH.

We were completely unaware that we were entangled in Satan's schemes and his evil ways. My focus was solely on myself, and that's precisely what he wants. I never even considered Satan's influence in our lives.

The concept of "dying to self" holds great significance in the Christian faith. It involves surrendering our own desires and will to live in alignment with God's will, not our own. Essentially, it means setting aside our selfish interests and submitting ourselves to God's plan and purpose.

Both of us were indulging in the desires of our flesh and pursuing our own wants rather than seeking what the Lord desired for us. We lacked the understanding of how to die to ourselves. John and I knew of God, but we didn't truly know Him on a personal level.

It was solely by God's grace that He saved us, not because of anything we had done. We weren't leading Christian lives within the confines of a church; instead, we were immersed in a sinful and wretched lifestyle at a clubhouse, strip joint and dive bars. Yet, despite our circumstances, He chose to extend His saving grace to us.

In Matthew 9:12-13 (ESV), Jesus declares, "Those who are well have no need of a physician, but those who are sick... I came not to call the righteous, but sinners."

I no longer dwell on the guilt or shame of where we once were. Instead, I focus on the beauty and blessings of what the Lord has done for us. He allowed these experiences to occur in our lives so that we could use them for His glory, and that is precisely what we are doing.

JOHN IS FREE!

The chains of evil fell to the ground, and it was a beautiful sight to behold. It wasn't just John's freedom from the MC that was significant, but the realization that through Jesus' work on the cross and His shed blood, John was forgiven of all his sins. We can define sin as anything that goes against God's will and law. It is inherent in human nature to have the inclination to sin, a consequence of the fall in the garden of Eden.

John understood that the next step for him was to be baptized. He desired to be obedient to God's calling. I had asked him to be baptized with me a year earlier, but he wasn't ready then. He used the same reasoning I did: "I was baptized as a child; I don't need to do it again." It's truly amazing how the Holy Spirit works in our lives when we are filled with Him. He convicts us and reveals to believers their righteousness in Christ Jesus.

Baptism itself does not save us. The Bible teaches that baptism is for those who have turned away from sin and have placed their faith in Jesus Christ as their Savior. Baptism serves as a testimony to the world that we have already been saved by God's grace through faith (Ephesians 2:8 ESV).

I could clearly see how God was at work in John's life. He began to pray and study Scripture to deepen his relationship with Him. John desired to hear from God and started experiencing thoughts and feelings that aligned with His will. He gained a better understanding of Christ and His significance in his daily life. John surrendered his life to God, finding relief in knowing that Christ died for his sins. John and I are truly blessed by God's grace, and it is knowing the extent of the Lord's sacrifice that sustains us each day.

Finding the right words to describe the feeling I had on the day John was baptized is challenging. It was the answer to my prayers, a precious gift from God. To be saved and chosen by Him is a beautiful blessing. Witnessing someone you love and have been praying for publicly declare their faith in Christ, in the presence of other believers, is a different gift altogether.

John and I went from frequenting bars and seedy places to attending Bible studies at friends' homes. Suddenly, we became acutely aware of the darkness that surrounded us for so many years. The transformation wasn't easy. It took time for John to grieve the loss of the friendships he had formed in the club. Though he knew deep down he wouldn't go back, the devil still attempted to tempt him, drawing him back into that world of darkness. But we serve a mighty God who protects us. He places people in our lives and along our journey to remind us of His truth, and for that, we are profoundly grateful.

There was a time when I mocked those who claimed to be "born again." I always felt that these Christians believed they were superior to me. Although I called myself a Christian, I did not understand what it truly meant to be born again.

I want to emphasize that I do not pass judgment on anyone's relationship with God. My intention is solely to share what is written in the Bible, hoping that it will provide the same help it offered me.

The term "born again" was first used by Christ Himself in response to a question from Nicodemus, as recorded in John 3:2-3 (ESV): "This man came to Jesus by night and said to him, 'Rabbi, we know that you are a teacher come from God, for no one can do these signs that you do unless God is with him.' Jesus answered him, 'Truly, truly, I say to you, unless one is born again, he cannot see the kingdom of God.'"

Being born again is not merely attending church or striving to be a better person. It is a life-altering experience. The things of the world no longer bring the same joy and fulfillment they once did. Jesus Christ becomes the focal point of every moment of your life.

Our close friends and family observed the transformation in our lives. The apostle Paul, the author of the book of Corinthians in the Bible, declares that when you are saved, you become a new creation. The old way of life passes away, and the new has come (2 Corinthians 5:17 ESV). When you accept Christ, you are changed by God, and He assumes control of your life.

The Holy Spirit, the third person of the Trinity, is often referred to as the "Helper" or "Comforter." He comes alongside believers to guide and empower them. The Holy Spirit convicts us of our sin, making us aware of how our choices may not align with God's will. He prompts us toward a life of repentance and reconciliation. His purpose is not to shame or condemn us, but to deepen our relationship with God. Conviction leads to confession and repentance, which ultimately leads to forgiveness and restoration.

I never experienced this kind of freedom before. Some of our friends and family feel uncomfortable with the change they see in us. They struggle to comprehend how we could put our faith and trust in Christ Jesus. They don't grasp the significance of sharing the gospel with everyone. Some doubt that this change will last, assuming it's only a matter of time before we returned to living for ourselves again.

I understand the belief in people's ability to change can be challenging for many. I, too, used to hold that perspective before Christ transformed my life. Without Him, we would be inclined to prioritize our own desires and live in a cycle of sin.

Following Christ is not always easy, as we will face judgment from the world. Some may even hate us because of our faith. That's why it is crucial to put on the full armor of God, as mentioned in Ephesians 6:10-18 (ESV):

> "Finally, be strong in the Lord and in the strength of his might. Put on the whole armor of God, that you may be able to stand against the schemes of the devil. For we do not wrestle against flesh and blood, but against the rulers, against the authorities, against the cosmic powers over this present darkness, against the spiritual force of evil in the heavenly places. Therefore, take up the whole armor of God, that you may be able to withstand in the evil day, and having done all, to stand firm. Stand therefore, having fastened on the belt of truth, and having put on the breastplate of righteousness, and, as shoes for your feet, having put on the readiness given by the gospel of peace. In all circumstances, take up the shield of faith, with which you can extinguish all the flaming darts of the evil one; and take the helmet of salvation, and the sword of the

PROPERTY OF THE KING

Spirit, which is the word of God, praying at all times in the Spirit, with all prayer and supplication."

By equipping ourselves with the armor of God, we are prepared to resist the schemes of the devil. Our battle is not against other people, but against the spiritual forces of evil. The armor consists of truth, righteousness, the readiness found in the gospel, faith, salvation, the word of God, and constant prayer in the Spirit.

Though the journey may be challenging, with God's strength and the armor He provides, we can stand firm and overcome the obstacles that come our way.

LIVING FOR CHRIST

During my time at cosmetology school, I was consistently advised to avoid discussions about politics or religion with clients if I wanted to achieve success. I embraced this advice and passed it on to my staff at the salon. Keeping our beliefs to ourselves became the norm as we followed the secular world's rules for a significant period.

However, my perspective on success has undergone a profound transformation. It is no longer measured by the balance in my bank account or the material possessions I possess. God gradually stripped away our attachment to worldly possessions. We decided to sell our cherished dream home on a sprawling ten-acre property and relocated to a comfortable residence in town. I parted with my car, and we now share a vehicle. Additionally, we sold our thriving 3,600 square foot salon and downsized to a smaller space, choosing not to employ anyone, except for a long-time friend who is also a sister in Christ, whom God made room for.

Our interactions with clients have taken on a new form. Christian music fills the salon, and we openly share our testimony and faith with those who visit. The intimacy of the smaller space allows us to engage in conversations with clients that were previously unattainable.

Instead of indulging in secular reading material, we immerse ourselves in the Bible and other Christ-centered books. Through this transformation, we have formed deep friendships with fellow believers, whom we consider not merely as a club, but as our brothers and sisters in Christ.

Even my social media accounts now predominantly reflect Jesus. Originally created as a platform to sell makeup, a Facebook group I established has expanded from a few hundred women to over 6,000 members and continues to grow. Instead of makeup tutorials, I now offer daily devotions, encouraging women to live purpose-filled, God-centered lives.

Looking back, I no longer recognize the person I used to be. Neither John nor I find empowerment in being served or respected; rather, we derive humility from serving and loving others.

This transformation occurred according to God's timing, not ours. When confronted with the ugliness of our struggles, the secular world's advice would have led us to a destructive path of divorce, allowing the devil to claim victory. But instead, both John and I turned to God during our darkest moments, and He redeemed us.

I am deeply grateful for the life we now lead. We have become covenant members at our church and serve in various capacities. John contributes to the safety team while I care for the children of the church during early services. Additionally, I have been invited to join the welcoming committee, akin to being a greeter at Walmart, but with a greater purpose.

God has instilled in us a desire to serve people in their life struggles, prompting us to enroll in Christian counseling classes. This education will also enable us to better serve our salon clients.

Our dream is to travel across the United States, sharing our story and testimony with those in need. Additionally, if it aligns with God's will, I aspire to write more books.

Reflecting on our past, it is astounding to consider the tremendous hardships our marriage endured, existing in danger and darkness with no hope. Yet, through God's grace, we transitioned from shame and guilt to basking in His illuminating light. Our testimony is a testament to His goodness and exists solely for His glory.

John and I are thrilled about embarking on this grand adventure, which we view as a divine gift. Although this adventure will eventually conclude when God calls us home for eternity. Until then, we wholeheartedly devote ourselves to serving our God. We pray to love our neighbors as Christ Jesus would. Undeniably, sometimes we stumble and backpedal, but the Holy Spirit swiftly works within us, reminding us of our identity in Christ. As Christians, our essence lies not in our sins but in our salvation through Jesus Christ. We are renewed each day and defined by who we are in Him, not who we once were.

Photo Gallery

Johnny and I at Tomahawk rally.

PROPERTY OF THE KING

Contemplating the life of an old lady.

I wore a property of cut everywhere we went. I use to think this was an honor.

DEBORAH MCKINZIE

A rare moment that John and I could take a bike ride by ourselves.

PROPERTY OF THE KING

Even when John wasn't physically with the club, he was always on his phone. I nicknamed him Hollywood.

DEBORAH MCKINZIE

In the rare moments when it was too hot to wear a leather vest, I always had some kind of clothing on supporting my husband's club.

PROPERTY OF THE KING

The picture that John sent me when he tricked me into believing he was arrested while he was in England.

John and I at Pretty Place Chapel in South Carolina.

DEBORAH MCKINZIE

John and I at a Christian Festival called Life Fest.

PROPERTY OF THE KING

John and I having dinner in Door Co., enjoying our best life, and all the blessings that God has given us.

From the Author

WRITING THIS BOOK HAS been an incredible gift to me. It has allowed me to release the ugly feelings I had been holding onto and let go of resentment. Through the experiences I've shared, I have learned invaluable lessons. I no longer feel the need to seek justice for the unfairness, abuse, or mistreatment I endured in the MC world. If justice is necessary, I trust it will come from God Almighty.

Gone are the days when I felt like a second-class citizen, burdened by guilt and shame. I have found forgiveness. Jesus Christ, through His sacrificial death, has purchased believers like me, setting us free from the bondage of sin. It is finished. God's grace has rescued and restored me.

It is important to note that I am no better than anyone else. This freedom is available for all His children to embrace and enjoy. As Galatians 2:20 (ESV) reminds us: "I have been crucified with Christ. It is no longer I who live, but Christ who lives in me. And the life I now live in the flesh I live by faith in the Son of God, who loved me and gave himself for me."

I share this story for the glory of God. He is good, and I pray that all my friends and even those who may consider themselves enemies find true freedom in Christ. The leather vest with the patched words

PROPERTY OF THE KING

"Property of" no longer defines my worth. I don't seek protection from a club to keep me safe, nor do I derive false power, strength, or confidence from anything that is not of God.

Today, I proudly identify as a Christian. I am the Lord our God's precious possession, clothed in the armor He provides. He shields me from the evil ways of this world. He will never abandon or forsake me because He loves me—and He loves you so.

We all need a Savior, and His name is Jesus. Let all honor and glory be given to God forever and ever! He is the eternal King, the unseen One who never dies. He alone is God.

Amen! Amen! Amen!

About the Author

DEBORAH IS THE AUTHOR of the inspiring book, Property of the King. Her journey to this point has been nothing short of transformative. It all began on a momentous Easter Sunday morning in 2017. It was then she had a profound realization of who Jesus truly was and the immeasurable impact of His sacrifice on her life. Embracing this revelation, she wholeheartedly surrendered her life to Him, setting her on a path of purpose and deep faith.

With over 30 years of experience as a cosmetologist, working alongside her husband and best friend, John, she has had the privilege of connecting with countless individuals and witnessing the power of transformation, both outward and inward. As God worked in her life, a strong desire to help women grow deeper in their faith and develop a closer relationship with God was birthed within her.

In her free time, she find joy in creative pursuits. Whether it's creating hairstyles, crafting beautiful beaded jewelry, knitting, or writing captivating stories, she cherishes every opportunity to express her creativity, no matter the canvas. Her dream is to embark on a journey with John and her beloved dogs, Leo & Boss, traveling across the U.S. and meeting incredible people along the way. They aspire to share their experiences, stories, and encounters, spreading inspiration and hope to all who cross their paths.

Learn more at:

deborahmckinzie.com

Acknowledgments

THIS BOOK'S CREATION IS a testament to the contributions of numerous individuals who have been instrumental in bringing it to life. My earnest prayer is that God's guiding hand will use this book to impact others, just as He guided me throughout this process. May He lead you to the opportunities and paths you have been praying for.

Foremost, my gratitude goes to my family. To my husband, whose unwavering encouragement and patient listening through countless revisions have made this endeavor possible. His support has been integral, and I couldn't have started this journey without his approval. This book isn't just about my life; it's about our lives together. To my parents, whose steadfast support, though they might not fully grasp the reasons behind sharing my personal experiences, has been a constant source of strength. Their upbringing with Christian values laid the foundation for me.

My heartfelt thanks extends to my son, Alex, who understood the times I had to cut short our card games to work on the book. His affirmations and love have strengthened me along the way.

To my cousin, Lisa Brouillette, whose tireless hours of editing breathed life into my words. Her unwavering belief in my ability and occasional nudges kept me going when the journey seemed daunting. Her strength, wisdom, and knowledge are truly inspiring.

As the book underwent multiple edits and received feedback from friends like Gina Wollner (thank you), God orchestrated the next steps. Josh Chadd, you've been an incredible gift. Your guidance in navigating the next stages was invaluable. You introduced me to Troy and Stacy Hooker, who contributed immensely to the book. From designing the cover, formatting, and more. Their contributions shaped the entire process. To Dawn Carter, your messages during the copy-editing phase were a source of joy and inspiration. I believe God gave me a new friend when you came into my life.

Kate Burie, your unwavering support, countless hours spent on web design, and coaching have meant the world to me. Your availability to share thoughts and your blessings are truly a gift from God.

To Pastor Alex, your presence in my life since my salvation has been profound. Your patience with my theological questions and unconventional ideas, your presence during both tears and laughter, have been a blessing. Your role in shaping the scriptural aspect of this book is deeply appreciated.

Melissa Inglese, my heartfelt gratitude for your enduring friendship. Your steadfast support and willingness to correct me when needed have been invaluable. Thank you for reminding me that God's timing prevails over my impatience. You've been by my side from the beginning, a friend and sister in Christ who's truly irreplaceable.

While it's impossible to individually acknowledge every person who has loved, supported, and prayed for me throughout this journey, please know that your presence has deeply touched my heart. To each one of you, I say, "To God be the glory!"

With heartfelt thanks,
Deborah Mckinzie